SleepWalking out of Afghanistan

Walking It All Back

D0862549

Harold Phifer

outskirts
press

Table of Contents

Introduction

AFGHANISTAN IS A war-torn country that's known for car bombs and suicide attacks. What is amazing is the fact that the country has almost no factories, no industries, no chemical plants--yet explosions are as common as catching a cold!

I found myself caught in the middle of the biggest vehicle explosion to ever hit Afghanistan. While dealing with injuries and destruction, my mind kept spinning out of control from horror to horror. Most of it revolved around my dysfunctional past. I did my best to replay my personal ordeals and the reactions of the people around me as accurately as possible. However, as I feared for my life, my complete history of existence kept bouncing back and forth in and out of my head!

Nothing about Afghanistan is comparable to anything that the average person can relate to or may have experienced! I tried to give a fair account of life as a foreign worker surrounded by unknown terrorists. After being in Afghanistan as contractors, only the fools, the desperate, and the greedy dare to return! Unfortunately, I fall into one or more of those categories! None of the events were a laughing matter and I didn't try to minimize any of our quests to survive.

The ventures of my life bounced like a yo-yo without a knot as I tried to come to grips with being at death's door! Once the characters are established you will find that most of my past is comically meshed together with abnormal circumstances. My stories take you through my highs and lows, while perhaps giving you some of the best laughter you will ever get from a book.

The journey starts out in the tropical country of Thailand where I was living a carefree life with no worries or drama. By happenstance I came across another retiree named Dylan that took advantage of my drunken state while easily coercing me to dive into my life history. It was a life that I buried deep below the surface—away from my kids, my family, my friends, my co-workers, and mainly myself.

After being forced to fight for my life, I had an avalanche of past events come gushing out from every possible angle. Dylan helped to open a door that took him and myself on a whirlwind tour like neither of us had ever expected or imagined!

There are so many twists and turns that feed into other stories or episodes. These features take place in areas like: Thailand, Afghanistan, Detroit, Louisiana, Oklahoma, Mississippi, Memphis, Houston, and back toThailand.

Like most confused males I had many good and bad relationships with the opposite sex. Yet I saw no real value in talking about my normal or balanced connections. Instead, I shared my many failures, embarrassments, and heartbreaks with the reader because it's just good entertainment and also a major part of my development. No doubt you will find them quite unusual and amusing as well.

Each brief story is sure to affect you differently than the previous one. Dealing with what I viewed as imminent death helped to bring closure to where I was once open and exposed.

The book touches on the sad, the shocking, and the schizophrenic behaviors that surrounded me until later in my adulthood. I tried to ratchet down those experiences with my sense of humor and my creative out-takes.

You will meet both male and female bullies throughout the book. You will get to follow my difficult and awkward approach to meet my dad. And finally, you will witness my hidden drive just to be loved and accepted.

I would hope that readers will desire to go back to these pages more than once. You may find yourself identifying with many of the events or characters. Hopefully, some of the stories will stick with you like nothing you have ever read or heard before.

Wagon Wheel on the Beach

ONE LAZY SUNDAY morning in Thailand I lost myself somewhere between watching bikini clad beauty queens decorating the beach and me being busy doing nothing. My days were full of kicking sea shells, throwing rocks, and counting the dolphins that leaped out of the ocean. Nothing around me was even remotely close to the world I left behind. To be honest I couldn't remember much about my past except the great adventures I had experienced. Not that I'm complaining! I was overjoyed to allow into my brain only the best of times. My go-to ritual was three margaritas for starters then the rest of my evenings were a blur and a smile.

Out of nowhere, I was approached by an older gentleman that missed his window for a massage just like I had. Dylan had been watching me for days as I policed the sand and coached the crabs back into the sea. I was keenly aware of his peering presence. I could tell that we were from starkly different worlds. Yes, the same country but my ventures in the U.S. and his connections were complete opposites. From that moment I held it against him. Living abroad had created a new perspective, but history is forever in your pores. So I wasn't quite feeling this surfer wannabe.

Most of the time I was spoiled in my own solitude and I assume he was also. Dylan had to be in his early 70's. He stood about six feet tall and was slightly overweight with frosty white hair. I could tell that he had a free spirit about him by his long salty locks and his half liter drinking mug. Paradise had taken a toll on this American. I have to say that Thailand had him in the mix of never-ending parties, sightseeing, and countless rows of level ten cuties! It wasn't hard to understand that Dylan saw me as company and a conversation that he badly needed. He really needed a friend. However, I was solidly sure I didn't need anything. My bygones were bygones, and I was ok with that! As for friends, I had none. I once had a dog but even he betrayed me. When I took him for a walk he waylaid our outing as an opportunity to flee from me! So Thailand was my new cover. It was a blanket like no other. As a matter of fact, if I was called home at one of these moments then, "Good Lord, let Thailand be the exit gate!"

Dylan boldly came up and asked where I was from and what brought me to this lovely country. Not wanting to spill my beans to a stranger, I flipped the inquiry on this nosy White guy.

"What brought you here?" I said. He told me that he was from New York. He was an ex-banker that had retired and decided to live abroad. He was a divorcee just like myself. His kids were successful adults, much like their dad. He was oozing with pride. It was his bio, yet I was beaming too! My kids were also unique achievers. He went on to say that he felt he needed a new lease on life so coming to this foreign land of sun, surf, and sand was his escape.

He must have noticed that I was fading in and out–distracted by the G-stringed girls.

He probed me once more as to how I'd gotten there. I begrudgingly turned toward him and said, "Dylan, my life had been in stages like the spokes of a wagon wheel. Each spoke may carry the same weight but they make up the many highs and lows of my mere existence."

Dylan gave a grin that sensed a gut-wrenching story from a drunkard full of deep doo-doo, but he said, "Continue on, my friend…"

I wasn't too pleased that he called me friend. I didn't know him nor was I looking for a friend. But the cheap hooch had worked its magic on me. I'd consumed more than my share! Something had to give. Either I could shower the beach with my dinner or I could give Dylan an earful of stories that glued me together like a sad stack of blocks. I chose to dump on Dylan.

I admitted that my highs started to spike upwards on a consistent basis in 2009. Until then life was a constant push and shove from day to day. Some things were my fault. Others were just consequences. And then there was the: "Oh God, what the Hell!"

Dylan snapped his head and asked me "What do you mean by the 'Oh God' thing?"

I said, "Dylan, I was a master at hiding who I was and where I came from. I went to Afghanistan for not only the money but as a way to escape the pain and humiliation of losing my kids, my friends, and my job! To be honest, people had always attempted to box me in. Even when things appeared above board there was always a hidden catch to my limitations. So leaving the U.S. was my way of getting outside of that loop."

Roadside bombs and suicide attacks happen all year round in Afghanistan. However, I somehow survived the biggest explosion to ever to hit that war-torn country. No, I wasn't ignorant to the possibility of being blown to shreds. But being in the middle of such an attack gave me a rewind that I wasn't prepared for."

The old man stood still and placed his hand over his mouth. With a soft raspy tone Dylan said, "We have nothing but tides and pelicans as our audience, so please explain."

I glared at the old fart and thought to myself that he must be a glutton for some crazy, crazy crap because I definitely had plenty of it! I told the old man that if he paid the tab then I would talk. I had been eating that heaven for days on end so why not peel back the pages? If he was going to fund my stupor then maybe it was time to unload the demons that owned me from start to present. Dylan quickly shot back, "You have a deal, my man" He reached his gnarly hand out and shook mine.

Back Together Again
Carey, "Take Me Away"!

I GOT A call from Quality Air Traffic Control in November 2009. The placement officer, Carey Lambert, assured me that he would bring me onboard if I wanted the job. That meant that I would be working as an International contractor. I had been waiting for a "new beginning" ever since I left Houston Air Traffic Control Center.

For three years I had been living in a broken down Recreational Vehicle (RV) with no running water, no air conditioning, no television, no toilet, no shower, and no internet! No doubt I had been in the more shadowy depths of Monroe, Louisiana.

When I left Memphis Air Traffic Control Center in 2000 for Houston, Texas I had no idea that my troubles would beat me to my new job. The scoundrels that wanted me out at my first facility also had connections at my new employment! Of course, I fought them like the beast from yonder but that war had far more knives in more places than I could match. Even though I won nearly every argument (about ten out of twelve) in my Equal Employment Opportunity Commission (EEOC) I heard the judge rule that there was not a pattern of discrimination! During those proceedings we uncovered lies by supervisors, falsified documents by management, and double standards toward yours truly. With that decision I was forced out through a naked and obvious reprisal. The FAA had won and a sound message had to be sent, with me being the example!

After getting pushed out I could no longer afford the life I had prior to my termination, but a Chapter 7 or Chapter 11 filing would have caused me to lose the bronze medal job I was assigned to. I had to hold on until I found another opportunity!

Each day I got up and headed to the one of my select hotels for a bird bath in the restrooms. Before returning to my shack I'd go to a different lodge for a Happy Hour meal. Those dinners were just appetizers that I had to overload on just to get a fill.

But I made a lot of friends amongst those establishments. Most of the workers saw me so often that they really thought I was a Diamond member.

Accepting the job with Quality ATC would bring a sigh of relief! Then I could make plans to reunite with my kids. It had been three years since I had seen my six-year-old son. His mom had gotten remarried and moved a thousand miles away. My child support was always on time but I didn't have the freedom or extra money to see him during my recovery! I worked six days a week. My rat-infested trailer was no place for my son.

I had not seen my nineteen-year-old daughter in as many years. I fell out of favor with her while going through the separation with my ex-wife. I blamed her for my sacrifices and my unplanned marriage to her mom. And in some ways I had made her responsible for the failure of our union. Suddenly, the hands of God had brought us back together.

My daughter was attending college in Kansas which was equally a thousand miles away from Monroe, Louisiana. She was on the basketball team. I had taught her most of her talents, but I was unable to see her play. Now that I was reborn I could go and be like the other fathers in the stands.

Turn Me On!

MY NEW BOSS, Albert Ogelsby, literally took me in just days before Houston Center put me on the streets! We were quite the odd couple. He was a deeply Southern White guy that had a love for hunting and fishing. He was a big country music fan and just a good-hearted man. He must have been chiseled out of Louisiana folklore.

I was a straight-laced African American that was more attuned to the big city life. I was more liberal, with a love for Jazz, Pop, and R-n-B music. Luckily, Mr. Ogelsby was a good judge of character. He put trust in me despite the garbage that my detractors placed at his feet. As I was advancing in my new position, Mr. Ogelsby sent me to Federal Aviation Academy in Oklahoma City for a skill-enhancement class. Oklahoma City just happened to be three hours away from my little lady. I would definitely go to see her and be the loudest dad in the crowd!

I had been to the FAA academy before but I didn't imagine I would be back in my wildest dreams! A lot had changed. The classes were smaller. I was in a new field of Air Traffic Control. I was learning a different skill like the "newbies." Even the jokes were different.

I had a female instructor teaching us how to sequence airplanes for landing. In the middle of her demonstration she told us how one pilot requested a "HARD TURN to FINAL"! That would be a sharp turn to line up to the airport. The instructor told the pilot, "I have a HARD TURN ON for you! How about IMAGINING ME in a DARK ROOM with BLACK PANTIES ON"!

I never gave any erotic instructions but I had fun acquiring new techniques.

A Opossum Is Still a Possum!

WHILE IN OKLAHOMA City I invited my daughter and my son to town for our big reunion. We stayed at The GREAT WORLD LODGE and WATER PARK. I spent the evening hugging the life out of my kids! I remember my son saying, "Dad, you are SMUSHING me!"

Of course he meant I was squeezing him much too tightly. It was super to feel like a "hands on" dad again! My son got his first boxing and wrestling lesson from me. He was a bit clumsy at times, yet he was all smiles. My daughter decided to get me caught up on her new jokes. She told me that she hated Opossums! I said, "Ok, I'll bite. Go ahead and tell me why!"

She said, "Not only do Opossums try to play dead but they also try to trick you with the way they spell their name" You know it's O-p-o-s-s-u-m-s and not Possums!"

My son was lucky to be at the Water Park when she told that sorry joke. However, he came into the lobby to tell me that one of the bigger kids had shoved him down. Just like any parent I had to ask "Why did the boy push on you?" My son told me that he wouldn't let the little boy's sister onto the water slide.

First, I admonished him for not being a gentleman to the little girl; then I challenged his toughness! I asked him, "What happened to the stuff I taught you the previous night?" With tears streaming down his face my son returned an emotional response of "Dad, that boy could have taken me out with just two shots!" Needless to say, I guess I did a poor job of mentoring him! He had to be recycled through my self-defense course before returning home.

Loving My Banker!

I WASN'T COMPLETELY sold on leaving the country and putting my safety on the line. I was still paying the bills. I was able to go places and take on dates like a normal man. My struggles had made me invisible but suddenly I was having relationship problems. That only meant that I was back on course! My world had gotten better faster than I had expected.

This time I was going to watch my Ps and my Qs. I was determined to do better things with my income. I needed a reliable bank for shelter and for growth.

Each day I would pass by the Big State Credit Union. It was a convenient and popular institution for controllers. Well, the problem wasn't the bank! The problem was Ms. Penny. She was the teller at that outlet. She was a different kind of creature. I had never seen anything as gorgeous as Ms. Penny! She was beauty and grace mixed in the same bowl. Just talking to her made me forget all of my intentions. I had to drive around the block just to recall who I was. After I returned I made a sizable deposit and signed her name! Ms. Penny corrected my error and sent me home to wait on her call.

Ms. Penny was a whiz with numbers. She was the head banker and the loan director. She even did my taxes. She kept up with my spending more than I did, and like a fool I didn't really mind!

It all sounded good until I realized that Ms. Penny was tracking me and following my money. She could tell where I had been and the things I bought. She always knew how much I had. My money had become her money. She told me that I needed a new car. She even approved the loan for a family station wagon even though I was a single man! She bought us a dog that she kept at her place.

Ms. Penny loved trouble as much as she loved my money. That was the ingredient that I initially overlooked. If we went out as a unit we would return as individuals. We were kicked out of clubs, bars, restaurants, and a couple of play pens. My pockets took the abuse of Ms. Penny's infractions and shenanigans.

The more I deposited the less money I had. If I wasn't buying, then Ms. Penny was ordering online. She would use my money to pay my debts only after she paid her bills! Ms. Penny had become a sum that I could no longer afford. Her math wasn't working for me. Ms. Penny was an expert at subtraction but allergic to addition.

It was time to dump her. It was time for me to close the books! The evil goddess didn't take kindly to my decision. She would hit me back where it hurts. She took my money and closed my accounts just to show me her power. She got me audited for years to come. She put the dog and her kids on me! The dog bit my wallet instead of my butt. Her runts took my gifts then said, "Talk to the hand!"

Once again I was broke and humiliated. Ms. Penny was charged with skimming the customer, yet I got very little money in return. Yes, I was making my way back but so were the scammers! I needed a better way out. I needed Afghanistan. The contract world was the start of my numerous adventures. I have since traveled to dozens of foreign countries! I have experienced unique cuisines. I have friends in languages that I don't understand.

Tick, Tick Boom!

I SAID,"DYLAN, I did accept the contractor job and I was cruising. I saw my new world as a beat of redemption. Quality ATC and the contract world constituted my new endeavor. There was no looking back. Going to a country at war didn't bother me either. Even when I interviewed for the job, I sold Quality ATC not only on my skills and experience but also on my good health.

I knew I had a keen awareness for picking up trouble and things out of the ordinary. That inner radar had been my protection from hostile entities for as long as I could remember.

The day the bomb hit I had a strange feeling that something was amiss. I couldn't put my finger on it. I kept staring at the guards, the cleaners, and the cooks, trying to get any insight to what was alarming me! It was around 3:00 p.m. We had just returned from work. I wanted to get a nap but I couldn't sleep. I just couldn't understand my restlessness! So I did a quiet walk around camp just to settle my nerves. After my short surveillance I returned to my room to lie down. I woke up for the 6:00 p.m. dinner. Being that it was still winter the darkness had set in. I foolishly decided to relax and let go of the uneasiness that bothered me earlier in the day.

I walked into the cafeteria, whereupon entering I saw Mike, Ace, and Jackson sitting closest to the door. Suddenly, there was a rumble and a simultaneous blast! This was no earthquake. It had to be a rendition of the Creation's Big Bang! The building levitated for seconds then slammed violently to the ground. The place went black as we were pelted with glass, asbestos, and wall plaster. The Taliban was known to blow the gate, followed by shooters that rushed in to kill as many as possible until they met their own demise. We had just witnessed "Phase One." The gunners had to be on the ground for "Phase Two!"

Jackson and me were thrown about twenty feet across the room but in the right direction. We landed next to a counter much like the walk up desk in the airport. We scurried behind it, drenched in debris. Jackson appeared ghostly white from the muck and plaster that covered him. I'm sure I appeared to be his twin. We were all gripped with anxiety. No doubt our time was up!

As we huddled behind the counter I looked at Jackson and he stared back at me. No words would surface. I took an immediate inventory of my faculties. I had two good eyes. The nose was intact. I felt no blood or wetness anywhere. I counted ten fingers. I was able to see my shoes and move my legs. So all functions were accounted for!

Our bearings were askew. We didn't know if we were coming or going. It was irony and embarrassment at the same time. Air Traffic Controllers are never lost. Air Traffic Controllers are always composed. But now we were the shaking lambs in the woods. We had not a clue as to the progress of the terrorists. Our dinner hall was at the back of the camp. If they entered from the front then we would be the last to be executed! But based upon the initial shock I would have sworn that they had breached through the ceiling.

I knew that when the Taliban crashes the party, then there's never ever any negotiations. You are going to meet your maker just like them. Rarely do they leave this world with a "soul to take"

So much was racing through my head. Things like, "How did I get here?" "Will I survive?" "Where is the help?" "How many of the Taliban are there?" "Will I see my kids again?" "Do I play dead?" "Do I go for broke and fight?" and "Am I ready to meet my God?" My emotions were clanging and crashing so hard that it flipped back all fifty-six years of my life. It was an "out of the body rush" that sent me back to my early days in Mississippi.

IF it was Mom, It was MAYHEM

HELLO WORLD

My first memory of existence was around the age of three. There stood my brother, Bennie, and me being restrained by one of the neighbors while his wife, Mrs. Brunson, and my mom were fighting throughout our house! Furniture was being rearranged to a designer's demise. A chair that was in the corner would be readjusted to the front of the room. A table that was once upright was suddenly upside down. There was nothing but fear and sheer terror engulfing the room! Mr. Brunson was chasing Bennie and dragging me around, as we tried to intervene in the fight!

The angst and hatred that Mom had for that couple lasted for about two decades.

I am not sure why they were enemies. I can only suspect that my mom had slept with Mr. Brunson. As disturbed as my mom was, and I mean a real whack job, I was completely shocked that she never got hurt! Nor did she inflict any apparent injuries upon anyone! At least not to my knowledge.

There were other heart stomping moments involving that couple! Another one that comes to mind was after the Brunsons had moved to another location. Mom found out where they were staying. She would fill some Coke bottles with kerosene, then depart with the intent to burn those people's house down. I can't describe the horror of thinking that my mom may harm someone! Or maybe she'd get injured or arrested!

My mom was a woman that had no filter. I don't think there was a barometer as to how low she would go to get revenge. I think the last kerosene cocktail incident occurred when I was about five years old. That time Mom took Bennie with her. I was praying and panicking because I was afraid of losing my mom *and* brother. After they safely returned, I quietly asked Bennie what happened. He said that Mom threw the bottles upon the Brunson's roof but nothing happened. I was relieved but I never knew if or when she would try again.

They Called Her Liza

MY MOM'S NAME was Eliza. She was called Liza or Ms. Liza. I recall seeing so many different reactions when her name was called. There would be snickers and sometimes laughter. But mostly looks of alarm and concern. It also depended on why her name was being called and what proximity you were to her.

She was so notorious that whenever the bullies were meddling, they would call my brothers and me "Little Liza"! When no one was around, the brothers and me would tease each other with the same "Little Liza" chant. It was like African Americans calling each other the "N-Word"! You had to be of the family to use that slur without being viewed as instigating a fight.

Rumors had it that my mom was given a spiked drink (mickey) when she was in her early twenties. From that moment it was said that she started doing weird things like talking to herself and lashing out at people without cause. I heard that story several times from unrelated sources.

Mom would talk and bark and bang items at home for hours upon end until she tired herself out. No doubt I was damaged by that behavior. I saw, heard, and witnessed things that would have made prison a nice escape from the antics that unfolded before me on a daily basis. There was no place to run. No place to hide. Jail would have been a more peaceful retreat. As far as I was concerned the rest of my relatives were Dodo birds as well. I mean there was no avoiding the foolishness that surrounded me. I thought about running away many times. But where would I go and how would I survive?

Often I would get into a verbal spat with Mom because she wouldn't pipe down! She was constantly arguing with the voices in her head. She would get more intense with her rambling, cursing, and banging if she thought she had an audience. Just when I thought I knew what to expect she would ad lib a new and more chilling twist to her show.

Around the age of ten, I would stupidly try to remove objects that were part of her showcase. But soon as I turned my back she would bludgeon me with anything nearby. I would grab my books and haul ass out of there! I would run to Aunt Kathy's (Mom's sister's) house. Little did I know that Aunt Kathy was the warden of that asylum. She would bandage me up, allow me to stay the night, but return me home the next day.

Neither Mom nor Aunt Kathy cared if my grades suffered as a result of that behavior. I wasn't the Golden Child and I certainly knew it! Bennie was the family's crowned jewel.

I wished and wished for a set of encyclopedias. Man, I could have gotten lost for days just between the pages! I knew if Bennie had desired them, it would undoubtedly have happened.

It got to where leaving wasn't even a consideration. I had to endure my situation until I went off to college. I rationally saw no other way out.

Of course, Aunt Kathy knew her sister was a lunatic but life was all about her and her superficial image. So deny, deny, deny was her angle. She would say to us that "Mom was crazy" but wouldn't admit such to anyone else. Aunt Kathy cherished the idea of Mom's derangement because it forced us to look up to her, especially her Bennie.

To Jail or Bust

MOM WAS WIDELY known as "THAT CRAZY LADY THAT RIDES A BIKE"! But before she acquired a bike she would walk everywhere. After Bennie started school I had to travel with Mom to and from work while my brother, Carl, would stay with a babysitter. Mom couldn't afford to pay a sitter for two kids . There was no daycare or "HEADSTART" (nursery for lower income people). Mom would walk at such a pace that I would beg her to slow down. The women with better employers would have someone to pick them up. My mom, being "the loose cannon," only got menial jobs. She always lost better positions because of her insane ways. So she had to get to her job by foot, which meant walking regardless of the elements. I had to take on those conditions as well.

On our journeys we would find all types of items to bring back home. Our house was the image of Sugar Ditch, Mississippi with a junkyard layout. It was certainly not a dwelling that would make the cover of "Homes to Go." Mom easily became a huge packrat. The house was loaded with her trash collections.

One day on our way from work we passed this landfill that was being leveled for future developments. The heavy machines were diligently at work. There were bulldozers and steam rollers all over the place. With me by her side, Mom went out amongst this chaos looking for anything of value. She started picking through this garbage that was being smashed and covered to make a new lot. The supervisor tried feverishly to get us to leave but Mom didn't care what or who was demanding that we exit the area. Suddenly, the cops arrived and took us downtown. We were thrown in a jail cell together until they decided what to do with us. This had to be around 1964. I was only four years old and I was staring out iron bars minus the jumpsuit. Our cell was down the hallway from the central desk. It was sort of like traveling down the walkway of an indoor storage unit. It was an isolated place; we were the only ones in holding at the time. As small as I was, I felt even smaller to see men in uniforms with guns, handling my mom and me. I can't begin to formulate the fright that possessed me! Jail was just something that I heard about or saw on television but now I was in the clutches of the police and who knows what? I kept looking at my mom and thinking, "Woman, what is your problem?" After about six hours we were released to Aunt Kathy. I fell asleep in the car on the way home, wishing it was all a bad dream.

Floyd Goes Bye Bye

WHEN I WAS around the age of five, Mom took Bennie, Carl, and me to Detroit by bus to see her brother, Floyd. That was her second trip to Detroit. On her initial visit, Aunt Kathy was the caretaker for Bennie until she returned to Mississippi. Bennie was a cute, light-skinned kid. He had a glowing smile that drew you to him. That's probably why I smiled so much. As a competing sibling, I must have been trying to imitate what got Bennie so much attention. Mom said when she returned to Mississippi that Bennie had grown attached to Aunt Kathy. He was even calling her Mom. Aunt Kathy was easily attached to him as well. Since she had no kids she decided to take Bennie as her own! Aunt Kathy had allegedly done so much for her siblings and, especially Mom, taking Bennie was just a minor down payment on Mom's perpetual debt. However, Mom wasn't having it! Mom had to get her brothers and sister involved to force Aunt Kathy to give her kid back. That defeat created a lifelong campaign as Aunt Kathy sought to prove that she was the better parent! She never passed up any opportunity to demean my mom in front of us or other relatives.

Uncle Floyd was the first man that I can remember showing me any real attention. As a matter of fact I haven't had too many hugs from any parent. Uncle Floyd was tough; he was a man's man! He talked to Bennie, Carl, and me with interest and affection. Bennie and me took that opportunity to tell Uncle Floyd about Mom's abnormal ways. We shared similar details with Aunt Kathy but nothing ever happened. The results were the same even after our talk with Uncle Floyd.

The cousins were about eight to ten years older than I. They were quite entertaining. We were their country relatives from Mississippi so it was a culture shock for them as well. We got to see snow and escalators for the first time. Unlike in the Bible belt of the South, stores were open on Sunday.

Mom was crazy but she was a momma bear when it came to us. Every other aspect of being a parent was totally lost, absent, amiss, and devoid with her. While in Detroit I had a run-in with one of my cousins. Mom chased this girl throughout the barnyard with the stick from a hog trough! No one messed with Liza's kids. In that case, Uncle Floyd did settle Mom down and comforted me too.

So we returned to Mississippi for what was a good adventure for me as a kid. A long bus ride home. A chance to see the countryside. But mostly time to connect with a solid adult (so I thought). A chance to be an individual where I wasn't just the side-show to Bennie.

It must have been the second day after our return that we suddenly got word that Uncle Floyd had been killed. Apparently, he and his wife had an argument and she shot him to death. Bennie and I never talked about it but I was shaken. Any closeness to death will especially shake a child I had bonded with this man. He saw my potential. He treated me as an equal, even to his own kids. He was someone I felt I could lean on as I grew up. It was all lost in an instant!

Only later in life did I learn of Aunt Kathy's control over her younger siblings. She would overtly tell them how to think and how to react. As presumptuous as I may sound, I do feel that she had a hand in Uncle Floyd's death!

Pray and Pray Some More!

DYLAN CHIMED IN and said, "Sorry to hear about your uncle, my friend."

I thanked him. The whiskey must have kicked in because I took lesser offense to being called "a friend." Plus, my focus was to rip off more bandages.

But Dylan interrupted. "Well, you are still walking amongst us." But the bombing had grabbed his attention. He asked, "What happened after you regained consciousness?"

I asked, "Dylan, what would you have done?"

"I think I would have crapped my pants and sobbed like a baby."

I chuckled and said, "Dylan, of course I wanted to cry. But the explosion happened so fast that it must have sealed all the crap inside."

He laughed a little but I felt a chill of remembrance! I was back behind that counter facing my worst nightmare.

I could vaguely hear Mike and Ace as they called out to Jackson and me. Everyone was ok except for the bumps and bruises. The bad news was that no one had a clue or plan of what to do. Unbeknownst to Jackson, Mike, and Ace was that I had been working "the Prayer Line" like a newborn Christian. I'm sure I prayed enough for all of us! Thank goodness the receiver wasn't off the hook. I know I confessed all my iniquities. I made promises and deals that I can never repay or live up to.

Other than our confirmation of survival, the silence of the room had all of us on the edge. We listened for help. We listened for horrors. I could only make out the popping of broken glass imitating gunshots. The waiting had made us delirious and an easy target. We needed to do something besides remaining stagnant until executed. The question was what and when? And who would initiate a move?

Out of the darkness eight Afghanis dashed out of the kitchen! They had pots and pans extended above their heads! They made a beeline through the aisles that separated the tables and headed out the back door screaming "la la la la la la!" I had no idea what that noise meant. I had heard similar chants coming from my mom. I just assumed "The End" had come, so I faded out for a fraction of a second.

When "The Walls" Talk Back

TO SAY THAT I had a love/hate relationship with my mom would be an understatement. I have to admit that I had a hate for her well into my twenties! I was the studious one. I was the ambitious one. And since I wasn't working, I needed her for school supplies, clothes, fees, and bus fare. I didn't dare participate in such activities as band or school clubs. I had to steer clear of anything that required money. Nonetheless, I had to constantly engage her until I found other means. That dynamic forced me to observe her tirades more than any of my other siblings because they had no great interest in school. Being that I stayed the course, I was mostly the solo rider in the Clown's car!

Mom was incessantly fighting with ghosts, devils, haints, and something she called "Dead Dogs!" She would be engaging "the walls with shouts, screams, and questions while exhibiting rage and con- tempt." She would even hold her ears as if she was waiting on "those walls" to respond! This would go on for hours until she exhausted herself or I did something moronic enough to break her rhythm.

When I attempted to disturb her, she would lock eyes with me as if to say, "Watch this" while she continued to bark, shout, scream, and bang "the walls" until she simply ran out of energy. Sometimes I felt sorry for "the walls" because she gave them pure hell! I had no idea what victory or satisfaction looked like for her. It was a neverending marathon. If she fought the the walls the previous night she would pick up the battle the next evening. Her howling constantly kept me up when I should have been in bed. Many times I would rush through my homework and leave the house. If I wasn't her victim at night, then she would make sure to embarrass me in front of my classmates before I caught the bus to school.

High school was about eight miles away. We lived in the poorest section of town. Most of the high schoolers from other venues caught the bus to school for free. Our community, the South Side, had to pay to ride the bus. It was the weirdest thing to me. We were the poorest district that fed into the school system, yet we had to pay whereas the more affluent school districts didn't have to. Many days I didn't have the thirty cents to ride the bus. Actually, it was sixty cents a day for both ways. Mom could not afford this so I had to be creative as to how I got to school. I would try daily to bum a ride to school. If I was unlucky then walking was the only way.

"Pop," The Weasel!

MOM WOULD DELAY leaving for work just to ride her bike past me and my schoolmates. I would freeze in shame and anger while maintaining the picture of normalcy to her and those around. I learned to hold quite a poker face. I was not going to let her know that she had an edge over me. I felt if she knew that she was getting under my skin then she would only do more drastic things. Without question, I took her best shots without blinking an eye. But on the inside I was saying, "Oh Holy God, this is Crazy as Hell!"

One of the biggest jokesters on our commute was this guy nicknamed "Pop." He had a sickness about his appearance. He was just nothing to look at. His speech was so muddled that you couldn't understand him. He was also a victim of polio. He had a terrible limp but he yearned for attention and laughter. He didn't need any prior preparation to take me on. He had unlimited material. The jokes he levied at me were better than any speech therapy at any cost. He would have the entire bus rocking and rolling in laughter! Others that he attempted to tease would punch him out, but I chose to take it. I was not going to beat up the handicapped. But, oh my, he was unrelenting even as I tried to stare him down. I would even throw harsh words his way but to no avail. Only an ass beating would shut him up! Yet, I wasn't going to go there. So some days I would intentionally miss my connection just to avoid encounters with Pop. And if I guessed right, I would avoid Mom riding her bike past our pick-up area! That became a cat and mouse game I had to play with her.

Those Dozens

MOM WAS ALWAYS the joke that only bullies dare mention. She would ride her bicycle to work, to markets, and to our schools whenever needed. She brought the laughs and the humiliations well beyond my deepest nightmare. I would fight or curse anyone that attempted to make fun of her. Yet the bullies would harass and humiliate me to the point that fighting wasn't a viable option. I was becoming just a tune-up or mere practice for those guys! So I had to learn to avoid them or absorb the insults.

I would judge my real friends by those who didn't take advantage of my situation with the jokes or silly remarks. That left only a few that cleared the bar. I was disassociating from people, even adults, like the plague. That invariably made me quite a loner.

Of course, kids will be kids. They would play a joke game called "The Dozens." This was a competition where kids would tell jokes about the other kid's mom just for laughs. It was easy to understand why everyone wanted to get me in that game. I would quickly leave the area because I knew the setup and for sure I wasn't going to win, no matter how funny I was. Even as I tried to sneak off a shot or two would be hurled my way. I had to just chalk it up as a victory for the bullies and the assholes! It was just a cross that I had to bear. All my peers knew my mom was the great equalizer. No matter how high I got, they could always crash me back down to earth by bringing up Ms. Liza and her exploits. Especially if I scored the highest on a test, there would be jokes or putdowns about Ms. Liza. Just anything to take the luster off being a step above them. And mostly I was smarter than they were, even with poor study habits, and no materials or books to enhance my knowledge. I was steps above them.

However, there was this one day when the tormentors kept me in the circle for a challenge of "The Dozens" even though I didn't want in. It was Crunch and Shank holding me hostage and pummeling me with jokes about my mom. They were the muscle guys that I definitely didn't want to fight.

Crunch fired shot after shot: He'd say, "If I need a spare tire I will call Ms. Liza. Hey, ask Ms. Liza if I can borrow her air pump? Someone tell Ms. Liza I need a ride to school" Everyone would laugh and scream!

Shank added, "Ms. Liza ran me off the road. Ms. Liza was popping-a-wheelie!"

Crunch came back with, "Your momma is the only lady on a bicycle to get a ticket by the traffic cop. I saw Ms. Liza burning rubber at the stop light." These guys were relentless yet scoring points (laughs) as in a video game.

Suddenly, I decided, What the Hell? I should go after these guys. So I started with, "Crunch, your momma beat me to the newspaper. I made Honor Roll but she was put on Hog Patrol!"

I said, "Shank, your momma applied to modeling school so they hired her at a trailer park as a double wide." Then I said, "Crunch and Shank moms put the mules out of business. All the farmers started using your mommas to plow the fields! After they got tractors they put your mommas out to pasture so they finally gave birth to you two asses."

I had turned the table and the laughs were coming my way! Without warning I was getting punches to my head and back from Crunch and Shank. I had to use my emergency escape to keep my injuries to a minimum. But Crunch and Shank would never try me again in the game of "The Dozens." They could talk it but they certainly couldn't take it!

Down But Not Out

I GOT INTO quite a few fights with my colleagues that were trying to put me down by making fun of my mom. It was a constant battle to shut people up. Or I was constantly trying to find some solace where either I was alone or the people around didn't know her.

One summer day I sat at the park observing the kids as they were playing and performing in their sports. At the time I was around fourteen years old. I was out watching the hotties as they went passing by. There was this girl named Ruby Dee with Down Syndrome that never spoke nor cared for me. She was in my immediate area hanging with the girls that I was watching. I knew she despised me because she would talk and laugh with everyone except me. On occasion, I would make attempts to speak but she would just stare back, roll her eyes, and say, "I know you're not talking to me!" Even though she was mentally challenged she had quite a personality.

I was normally quiet and reserved but that day I was out to chase. I was being flirty and the responses were promising. Lucky for me, so I thought! Suddenly a couple guys apparently became jealous or curious. They stepped forward and started teasing me about Ms. Liza. I tried to blow it off but they were intent on breaking me. The cuties laughed and headed off. Now I was embarrassed and peeved so I gave warning that the "ass beatings were about to start."

At that point I was determined to place my foot in someone's rear end! Everyone scattered with screams of "Ms. Liza, Ms. Liza" as they dashed away, but taking those last parting shots. The only person left within striking range was Ruby Dee. She stepped to my face whereas everyone else was watching from afar. With composure and with confidence Ruby Dee stammered and stuttered her statement: "Your mom–momma is Ms. Liza, Now! Your mom,—momma ride ri–rides a bike!"

What a dilemma! Normally, I would have punched "A regular John." Or I would have cursed and belittled "Any other Jane." But Ruby Dee was a female with Down Syndrome! First, I wouldn't hit a female at my mature age. And secondly, I would have looked like a rambling idiot to stand there and trade insults with Ruby Dee. Undoubtedly, I allowed restraint to rule the day! As I locked eyes and gave Ruby Dee a smile, she went on to say, "Buster, get to stepping!" She was feisty and not feeling me at all. Score one for Ruby Dee. I was initially pushed to the brink of planting a foot into someone's behind but Ruby Dee's toughness kept my feet on solid ground.

Exit Stage Left!

I HEARD DYLAN trying to imitate Ruby Dee with "Your mom–momma ride ri–rides a bike." I gave him one of my stare downs and I told him, "The crap wasn't funny then and it ain't now."

He clenched up and said, "Sorry, man."

I said, "Dylan, I was just screwing with you! If I didn't think it was funny then I would not have brought it up."

Dylan was traveling back in history with me but my near death encounter was heavily on his mind. He moved from teasing me to asking what happened when the Afghani came dashing through the aisles.

I said, "Yes, we were white-knuckle scared of our impending deaths, only to realize that these guys were the food servers. That wasn't exactly the best predicament either because we never knew who to trust. There had been many incidents of "Green on Blue" attacks! The maneuver of running out of the lunch hall could have been a setup to get us to come out of hiding.

Mike, Ace, and Jackson went for it. They followed the servers out the door! I gave the room one final look over and joined my coworkers through the exit. Even though I was the oldest I was still no slouch athletically compared to my colleagues. But they had left me in the starting blocks as if I was asleep when the referee said, "Go." As I got to the exit door no one was in sight! They had all made haste to the "safe room." Yet, I was taking no chances. Before I left the building I stopped to get a sense of what was out in the mist and if I was being targeted! I saw nothing. The popping of glass became much more

31

audible. However, I had no way of knowing if it was glass or gun-shots. I was all alone! I entered through the door of my dormitory as quietly as possible. I was getting closer to my designated shelter. Yet, it seemed like miles away. I felt something wet streaming down my leg! Without realizing it I had scraped the twisted medal south of the door handle, creating a gash in my left leg. This was similar to the cut my mom had given me back in high school.

The thumping of my heart became louder and more intense. I was hyperventilating as I crumbled to the floor and out I went!"

Like Magic: A Saw

I OFTEN WONDERED why we were never taken away from Mom and placed in foster care. Anything would have been better than the humiliations, the lack of love, and lack of attention we received. Mom wasn't equipped with the ability to mold us or push us forward! She even told us to not call her "mom"! With that statement I felt, "The Walls" going up! She didn't hug or kiss us either. I learned quickly to hide my emotions. I knew to pull myself together regardless of how dire my situation was! I have tried to describe this to my own kids. Not that I want them to be as tough as I was but to understand that I lived a life of very little emotion. I never had a shoulder to cry on. I never had someone to whom I could lay out my fears, my doubts, or my insecurities. Someone to tell me, "Baby, it's going to be all right!" Or, "Baby, God wants you to pray about it!" I learned to accept or resolve my own issues, then attempt to keep stepping forward.

It didn't take a genius to realize that we represented income to Mom. So letting go of us would have meant losing welfare money. If I wanted to quit school in elementary she would have never said a word. I'm pretty sure that my Aunt Kathy would have said even less, especially since I was not her Bennie. As a matter of fact, all of my brothers quit school around the 9th grade. Mom didn't take any issue with that. For her it meant no more responsibility for those kids. They could work and fend for themselves.

I was the lone holdout. I was becoming quite a problem for her. When I got to high school I chose not to work regularly. That was a move that would cost me dearly when I got to college and desperately needed a job. By taking myself out of the market I had no real work history. The expenses of high school and me being a growing boy kept mounting day after day. The more I was home the more Mom would bark and howl at the voices in her head. Each night her displays would reach such a peak that I was baffled that our neighbors never called the cops! We lived in the projects where there were families to the left and to the right of us. Plus, we resided on the second floor where there were families underneath us as well. I guess it was the general fear of mom that kept our neighbors from calling the police.

The last time I took matters into my own hands was when I was seventeen years old! I grabbed Mom's noise makers while stating that she needed to "Stop this crazy mess!" Yes, I knew that was a bad, bad move but I just couldn't take another sound! As I mentioned previously, Mom was a collector of all things left on the road. And did I know that she had added a table saw to her collection? Certainly! But a number of other items were jarringly disturbing! After I cleared the area of her homemade symbols and percussion instruments I stepped into the restroom. Like a light switch being toggled off, the house fell silent. I was vainly thinking, now I can read and waltz off to bed. It had to be around midnight at the time. I had school in the morning. As I stepped out of the bathroom I was blindsided by a table saw gouging a hole the size of a quarter in my left hip. Mom had retaliated and I was too foolish to have expected anything less. I grimaced in pain as I felt the blood gushing down my leg. I grabbed my coat and headed to Aunt Kathy's house for the rest of the night!

Now You See "The Hen," Now You Don't

BEFORE I GRADUATED high school I let it be known that I registered for college. Mom threw a "cursing fit-fest" because I was not pursuing a job to bring money into the house. Sorry, I thought. This was finally my chance to get off that crazy carousel! I was returning my Broadway tickets. Nothing was going to stop my entry into college. Mom would increase her disgust for me because of that decision. It really didn't matter because I had resentments against her as well!

I don't recall what Mom's last shocker was. To be honest I'm sure it was far more than I ever wanted to know! However, I found out while I was away at school that Mom had been arrested for stealing a frozen chicken from the grocery store. I was thinking that mom was many things but not a thief! Now that label had to be added! Here, I was an adult of twenty years. I couldn't help but think how poor of an example she had been. I had been forced time after time to find strength to get past her zaniness. But I had nothing left to hold onto. There was just nothing more to give me insight. I finally resolved to see her as little as possible! I needed to move on in order to preserve my own sanity.

Deliver Us from Aunt Kathy: My Hero

I GREW UP knowing I had burn scars covering thirty percent of my body. Luckily, I was spared the good parts! Of course I had a complex about my patches until my late twenties. Then I finally viewed them as a badge of honor. I have even gotten compliments about my scars!

The story I was told was that Mom had a "hot plate" (electric burner) on the floor with boiling hot water that was left unattended! As an infant I bumped into that heater, spilling the hot liquid onto my fragile body. Aunt Kathy rushed me to the hospital where I stayed until able to return home. I held that against my mom for many years for being so reckless!

I told one of my college buddies about my ordeal. He turned it into a joke and I guess I was ok with it. He said, 'It may have been water but it could have been fire the next time!" I had to admit that was a good one.

Aunt Kathy took advantage of that situation. She indebted Mom and me with her heroine service. All of my interactions with her were followed by her words, "You all really owe me a lot" or "Yaw'l got to pay me back." She felt that we should be obligated to her forever! It was a chain that crippled me like shackles to an elephant. We were just compelled to work for her like servants at the drop of a hat.

I was short and very skinny for most of my childhood. My teeth were brownish with indentations. No doubt I was a malnourished child. When it came to food Aunt Kathy had plenty of it. I'm not sure where she got it all but food was everywhere. She had two loaded refrigerators and two loaded freezers. She had preserves, fruits, nuts, canned goods, potato chips, and candy just laying around the house. She wouldn't allow us to take any of it. Fruit was never eaten and would simply rot. Only Bennie could ask for and receive those delights. The opportunity for food was one of the reasons I would volunteer to help Bennie with Aunt Kathy's assigned chores. I knew Bennie could get me snacks when the jobs were done!

Dog Poison

IT TAKES TIME, patience, attention, and love to care for an animal. Aunt Kathy had none of those qualities. She would get a dog just because it was available. After obtaining a dog it was always a sad affair for the pet and its arrangement. The poor dog would be tied to a stump on a short leash where he had to eat and crap almost in the same area. There would be poop two to three feet high almost next to the dog's drinking bowl. She would feed the dog the same food that was meant for a pig but not good for a canine. The helpless creature was always sick yet she wondered why! There was no walking the dog, grooming the dog, or taking the dog to the veterinarian! If her dog got free he was off to the races like a fugitive on the lam. And if he didn't escape he would eventually die from his prolonged closeness to his own manure! Looking back, those defectors were far smarter than I. I definitely should have followed their lead and gotten the hell out of Dodge!

No Opening Acts Wanted

MY BROTHER, BENNIE, was three years older, handsome, energetic, and quite the attention-getter. He was everything I wasn't! I was the dark skinned kid with what I would call a "normal" look. There was nothing special about my appearance that would draw you in. However, I was inquisitive and a sponge for information! My drive annoyed everyone whenever Bennie was around. Bennie was the kid they all wanted to get next to. On the other hand; Bennie was as dumb as a lump of wood. He always sought attention but had no interests beyond being praised and pampered. Aunt Kathy would invite her friends and relatives over to see her adorable nephew. Bennie would dance, smile, sing, and everyone loved it! I would dance, smile, sing, and Aunt Kathy would ask me to move out of the way. I thought of us as little dancing bears. But in reality I was a terrible substitute for the main event.

I taught myself to read before the age of three. Bennie struggled to read well into the 2nd and 3rd grades. Before I started school Bennie and I spent a lot of time at Aunt Kathy's house. I would do Bennie's homework on a daily basis. However, when I started school I rarely saw Bennie. Aunt Kathy would scoop him up and take him to the supermarket, to the county fair, or to church conferences. Subsequently, Bennie failed the 4th grade. Aunt Kathy blamed Mom for Bennie's collapse. If anyone was to blame it was Aunt Kathy. Plus, I wasn't around to dabble in Bennie's schoolwork.

Aunt Kathy hated anyone that dared to befriend us. It was tough having a connection outside of her, Mom, and my brothers. Her advice or encouragement always left me empty and bewildered. She would say things like "You don't need to join the Boy Scouts because they don't know what they are doing" or "the school play is just a bunch of foolishness." I had interest in those activities but not Bennie.

Listen to My Gun

AUNT KATHY WAS the matriarch of the family. She claimed to have raised the other aunts and uncles. However, she was the oldest and her siblings did bow down to her. Even I looked up to her more than I did my own mom. At the age of twenty I finally saw the demon of her ways! After that I kept my distance as much as possible. But in retaliation she was determined to "get me" or "show me" what happens when people blow her off!

Mom allowed Aunt Kathy to control her and her world. That meant Aunt Kathy controlled Mom's kids too. She even named all of Mom's kids.

Many times Mom's boyfriends would stay over for the night. If a man was around when Aunt Kathy came by, she would berate him and throw him out. I even saw her toss guys out at gunpoint! She'd threaten them by saying, "I will shoot you until I can't see you!"

I remember thinking, "How is that possible? That's a lot of damn shooting!" But Mom never stood up to Aunt Kathy. She would just invite her men back over the following night.

2 Wheels Only

AUNT KATHY MADE almost all major decisions that went on in our household. She simply treated Mom as less-than-nothing from my childhood to the day Mom died.

Mom made the mistake of telling Aunt Kathy of her desire to buy a car when I was five years old. Secretly, I was afraid of Mom getting a car, but I was a kid and cars did excite me. Plus, I was tired of trying to keep up with her on our walks to her jobs. Mom, Aunt Kathy, and me would go out for a test drive. From a kid's viewpoint Mom did remarkably well. Aunt Kathy not only killed the deal, she also took a large portion of Mom's car money! Aunt Kathy always had to get her cut. She even knew what was in Mom's bank account at all times. Aunt Kathy would constantly probe me regarding if or when I sent money home. Whenever she guessed correctly she would show up just to demand a share. After Mom failed in her attempt to get a car she went out and bought a bicycle. She would ultimately become "THE CRAZY LADY THAT RIDES A BIKE."

Sister 2 Sisters

MOM HAD ANOTHER sister named Betty who looked strikingly like her. Aunt Betty and her husband, Willie, invited us out to their home in West Point, Mississippi around 1966. They had quite a bit of land compared to our rented shack in Columbus. As the cousins were showing Bennie and me the animals on the farm we heard a lot of commotion coming from the house. Mind you the cousins were four to six years older than Bennie and me. We hustled back to see what was going on! As we returned Aunt Kathy had Mom on the ground in a fight! And like deja vu, Bennie and me were being restrained by Uncle Willie, Aunt Betty, and our cousins. It was like a recurring nightmare! There I was again struggling to stop an attack on my mom! While Aunt Kathy was dragging Mom by the hair she was also threatening to beat my ass if I continued trying to intervene! She had beaten my ass many times before for things that were much smaller in nature. Yet I can't recall her or Mom ever whipping Bennie. Trust me, up until that point Bennie and me had gotten into a lot crap together! There was no "good kid" or "bad kid"! We were just a mischievous tandem. The ride back to Columbus was ghostly quiet and uncomfortable for Mom, Bennie, and especially me. I kept thinking the whole time that I had a butt beating coming my way!

The Car Made Me Do It

BENNIE AND ME grew apart due to the time he spent away from Carl and me. Plus, Aunt Kathy programmed him to think he was so much better than us. Bennie arrogance showed repeatedly toward Carl and me. He would constantly fight me without a moment's notice because I would challenge him on his stupidity and his sucky attitude. After getting bruised I would retreat to Aunt Kathy for support and bandages. As usual she would return me home but said nothing to Bennie about him strong-arming me.

Since Mom rode a bike, there wasn't ever a car in the household to go anyplace or do anything. We were always at the mercy and disdain of other drivers! There wasn't anyone around who cared enough or was crazy enough to allow me to get behind their wheels! So during my freshman year at Mississippi State I devised a plan that allowed me to save some of my college funds. I took extreme measures to reach my goal of buying a car. Such sacrifices as borrowing books instead of buying them. Eating peanut butter sandwiches instead of getting a meal ticket. I took that money (around 1000 dollars) and bought a 1972 Ford Torino. Of course I could not drive nor afford the insurance. But this was Mississippi where there was no law requiring car insurance. I knew that once I bought a vehicle I would eventually teach myself to operate it. The day of my driving test no one asked me how I got to the Department of Motors Vehicles (DMV). That was a lucky break for me!

After Bennie saw I had a car he sparkled with excitement as if it was his car too! He normally would wear my clothes without asking.

I never said much because he was my big brother. Being that I had grown three inches taller, he could wear my clothes but I couldn't wear his. So, it was somewhat a given that he would assume that he could use my car as if it was his car as well.

One Friday evening I had planned a night out on a date when Bennie asked if he could use my car. I told him sure as long as he was back by 6:00 p.m. As time passed I kept checking outside to see if he had made it back. The closer it got to 7:00 p.m. the more I was pacing up and down the street to see if Bennie was coming around the bend. About eleven hours later Bennie arrived home as drunk as a sailor on a Saturday night. I was pissed! I had missed my date and Bennie had taken the utmost advantage of me. I was getting more hysterical by the minute. I said, "Where in hell have you been?"

He murmured a couple of incoherent sentences.

I said many curse words and just "DAMN, DAMN, DAMN," to him and myself! I went outside to check out my car. As I turned the engine over and started to take off, the car rose then dropped. Something wasn't right. I got out and looked at the front end and noticed that both tires were pointing outward. The car was not drivable because the axles were broken. I raced into the house and said to Bennie, "What have you done to my car?"

He told me, "Your car caused me to get a ticket!" Then he caught me with a sucker punch. I landed a couple of good shots but it was no use. He was drunk and I needed to try to avenge my frustrations when he was sober.

I couldn't help but ponder how the cops allowed him to drive home in his drunken condition. After racking my brain trying to recreate the pieces, I surmised that he had a drink or two then drove over the curb, breaking the car axles. That had to be why he got a ticket for running over the curb or he drove over a traffic sign which would also explain getting a ticket and breaking the car axles. After being released he then stopped at a bar to get liquored up. He left the bar, waddled back and forth, but successfully mads it home.

In an attempt to show his independence Bennie went out and bought a 1970 Pontiac. I asked him how much he paid for it. He told me $200. All I could say was 'ok' with a grin. I didn't think he would get much out of his bargain car. He didn't! His Pontiac ran for one day only and I never saw it move again!

I Saw What She Was Working With

BENNIE NEVER GOT past being prohibited to drive my car. But I didn't really care. I had a major disdain for him! I was still upset about his attack on me! I was still fuming about his destruction of my car. He still showed an utter disrespect for me as well. To say I was premeditating a fight would have been a correct assumption. Sooner or later I knew he would take the bait, and I was going to gain some satisfaction over him.

Just as I had planned Bennie started a fight over something that was all so frivolous. But that was just who he was. He was the young male version of Aunt Kathy. He would boss us around and take whatever he wanted. Bennie's reign had come to an end! I beat his butt like a busted punching bag!

This time Bennie retreated to Aunt Kathy. He tattled as much as he could muster. He said that I wouldn't allow him to drive my car. He told that I had beaten his butt! He told that I was making my youngest brother, Tommy, attend school. That was something that I thought was an admirable thing! Still I wasn't looking too good compared to her "golden child." Not to be forgotten, I had ended my servitude to her since 1980.

Unexpectedly I got a visit from the great Aunt Kathy on a Sunday morning. She was a big Christian who never missed church. So I was caught completely flat-footed. Bennie must have tipped her off that I was in town! It was a weekend that I had come home from college as a respite from school and to check on my younger brothers. Aunt Kathy walked in and turned off my professional football game. She told me, "I hear that you have been acting up!"

I was baffled as to what she was referring to! It had been more than a month since Bennie and I had our skirmish. Regardless, she continued on, "You are not dad to anyone here," she said. I was sitting on the bed and completely on mute. Finally, she said, "If I have to come back here , it won't be pretty!"

She flashed me her Saturday Night Special before returning to her Sunday service! I looked at her and mindlessly gave a little smirk. In actuality I was totally jolted and hurt that she would threaten me with a weapon! I had never had any confrontations with her. Yes, I did avoid her! But staying away was only recent versus all of my twenty years. I had never done or said anything disrespectful! I had never given any lip service, or rolled my eyes, or turned a blind eye.

My run-in with Bennie was the first time that I was ever on the winning end! After she left, it dawned on me that her display was all about Bennie and nothing else. Messing with Bennie was what sent her over the edge! She was so determined to smash me that she sacrificed Tommy's well being. After she punked me down, Tommy would quit school and join the delinquents that he was aspiring to be. I was awakened like never before.

Panic Room At Last!

DYLAN WAS SUDDENLY compelled back to my terrorist account in Afghanistan. He asked me, "Did you pass out in the hallway?"

I said, "Yes, I did for a split second." Blood had rushed to my head so fast that I had to stop to pull myself together. I regained stability by hugging the walls of our dorm. My room was across from the "Safe Area" on the second floor. I inched closer. I needed to climb the stairs to have hope of survival. The hallway was dark, empty, and deathly silent! I walked ever so gingerly. I must be alert to any noise of oncoming killers! Plus, I didn't want them to know I was roaming about. I made it to the steps, but stopped before ascending upwards. I wanted to peep and listen for any threats without exposing myself. I heard nothing. I crept up the stairs where I found numerous contractors lying on the floor in triage. I was relieved to be among humanity even though they were so injured from that nightmare.

People were just in a daze. No one looked normal. Most of the injuries were scrapes and deep cuts due to the compression created by the explosion. No one was really speaking. Nearly everyone appeared lost.

I had made it to the shelter but I still felt vulnerable and cold. I sat back on the table as the nurse examined me. I tried to go to a "happy place" but I was back in rewind.

Even the Devil Needs a Heart

IN 1998 AUNT Kathy needed a quintuplet bypass operation. To that date I had never heard of more than a quadruple heart surgery. I didn't have the highest of confidence in her survival. She had to be about 73 years old. It just wasn't looking good as far as I was concerned. But she had an air of determination! She wouldn't even entertain the conversation of "What if?" I told myself that I should bury the hatchet and be the best I could be. That was exactly what I did. I was very attentive. I was there in the morning before work and at night after work. I prayed with her time and time again. When I was alone I did shed some tears. She was the only family I had known all my life. She was the only person that Mom really cared about. Mom loved her dearly. I knew she didn't care for Mom but now was not the time to think of her shortcomings.

She gave me phone numbers of people that she considered to be close to her. These people would include Uncle Dan, a church member, and Pastor Lloyd.

Uncle Dan was her youngest and dearest sibling. Aunt Kathy and Uncle Dan were like Satan and Damien. They did evil that only the Devil could understand. Aunt Kathy had such influence over Uncle Dan that he failed to love his own kids. Uncle Dan had six girls yet he showed love to only the youngest daughter. Aunt Kathy would mirror his lack of affection for his kids. Uncle Dan's wife had taken ill when I was about ten years old. She would never return home to be with the kids. Uncle Dan became the cousins' sole caregiver for the rest of their childhood. He restricted the girl's desire to communicate with one another at any time. Aunt Kathy had to have known about his behavior. I am convinced that she even encouraged it.

Uncle Dan and Aunt Kathy went so far as to will their possessions over to each other. Aunt Kathy signed her property over to Uncle Dan and he signed his property over to her. They wanted to make sure that none of Uncle Dan's daughters got access to his belongings in the event of his death. Aunt Kathy wanted to make sure that no one in my family got access to her belongings except Uncle Dan.

I would first place a call to Uncle Dan. When he answered the phone, he was eerily silent. I told him of Aunt Kathy's impending operation. He asked no questions nor requested any updates. I got the impression that I was only interrupting something!

Next, I called Pastor Lloyd. Pastor Lloyd had been the minister of our church since 1965. Aunt Kathy loved this man as much as God himself. As the congregation would exit the building she'd place her offering directly into Pastor Lloyd's hands. As I spoke to Pastor Lloyd, he was so quiet that I wondered if he was still on the phone. There was no "Praise the Lord" or "Trust in God!" There was no "me and my flock will be calling on high for her recovery." To say Pastor Lloyd was without words best describes that encounter. Once again there were no questions or requests for phone numbers, or her room numbers. He didn't even ask what hospital she was at. Admittedly, I was totally startled by the responses of Uncle Dan and Pastor Lloyd.

I called the church member and their reception was more prayerful and of more concern. Finally, I called my brother, Bennie. He listened but said nothing! I told him of my unprofessional prognosis for Aunt Kathy. Still he gave no reaction nor did he request any further details.

The night before her operation I called all those people once again. In my head this was their final chance to say something before Aunt Kathy passed. I got the same reactions from Uncle Dan and Pastor Lloyd. I then called Bennie (our golden boy and Aunt Kathy's fantasy son). He was dismissive and somewhat bothered that I had even called. He hung up on me! I dialed right back and gave him the riot act. I told him that his aunt had always been there for him and that he could at least talk to her! He just said, "Uh huh," and hung up again. I called him back a third time and I told him that he was "a piece of crap" but he cut me off with a final click click click, probably before he heard the "crap" word!

Aunt Kathy would make it through surgery. She would reach out to the people mentioned beforehand to notify them that she was ok. I never told her of the responses I got from Uncle Dan, Pastor Lloyd, or her Bennie. However, it dawned on me that Aunt Kathy had been such a terror and a disruptive force that the church didn't care if she lived or died! As for Uncle Dan and Bennie, I know nothing to explain their dismissive behavior.

For a short time Aunt Kathy was a totally new person. I would even say that she was humanlike! She was giddy and remorseful at times. The experience had even changed me. I had little faith regarding her survival. I had watched that old Christian pray and pray when hope was bleak. Not only had I witnessed it, I was genuinely there in mind and in spirit!

Out of guilt Aunt Kathy wanted to give me money. I kept telling her that she owed me nothing. She was persistent so I told her that I would accept the money only if she called it a loan. It was so weird because I didn't need it. But to soothe her I took it and paid her back three months later.

Bennie Takes a Bride

MY BROTHER WAS quite the ladies' man. As the cliche goes "it was good that he was handsome because he had nothing else to offer." But his smile was magnetic. I couldn't help but be jealous. His looks always got him the hot chicks. Plus, he wasn't attacked for being "the kid of the Crazy Lady that Rides a Bike." People like Aunt Kathy would shower him with gifts, money, and trips beyond anything that I could imagine. Being his brother did bring some interest by association but that was where it ended. I got to know quite a few "pretty boys." They had more of a fraternal connection to each other. I got to see "the magic" close up. When I heard jokes of me being the "ladies' man," I was flattered but my relationships with females were laughable compared to the "real pretty boys" I came to know.

In 1979 on a trip home from college, Bennie informed me that he was getting married the following weekend. I was taken aback because it was on such short notice. So I asked where the wedding would be held. Where was the honeymoon? Where would they reside? He told me the wedding was at his bride's house and he planned to live with his bride's family. I was stunned silly, but nothing he had ever done had been logical so why should things make sense now? I took a deep breath and told him I would try to make it. No promises but I would definitely do my best!

The next weekend I got to Columbus the morning of the wedding. I had only one suit. Of course, I thought I was the cat's meow whenever I put it on! The funniest thing was that I actually bought that suit twice. The first suit was destroyed initially by Bennie. Unbeknownst to me he sneaked the suit out of the house and wore it to a bar. His drinking had become a problem. Alcohol gave him "liquid courage" that he otherwise didn't have. He got into a fight and the material was ripped beyond repair. He wasn't responsible enough to replace it so I scraped up enough money to buy the same identical suit.

As I went through my preparations for the wedding I was thunderstruck to find that my outfit was missing! Bennie had taken my one and only suit once again without permission. I was so peeved I decided against attending the wedding.

Bennie went on to get married. He would move in with his bride and her family. Because of his abusive drinking and tendency to fight I feared for what could unfold at his new home. He was the type of idiot that would fight with his wife at the drop of a hat! He was even more likely to fight with her in her own home. Sadly, his first marriage didn't last very long.

Around 1990 I got word that Bennie had remarried. I hadn't seen him for some time so I had to do my own discovery to find out where he was living. I gave him a call to alert him that I was in town and I would be stopping by to see him. When I got to his duplex the lady that answered the door was someone that I can best describe as the "sidekick of Big Foot"! I was polite or maybe cautious as I proceeded to the back room where he was sitting. The years of drinking had taken quite a toll on him! He was not even close to the handsome man he once was. He asked me if I had met his wife, Barbara, at the door! I nearly pissed my pants! There was nothing endearing about this lady. She wasn't a looker, nor shapely, nor personable. How in the hell had this happened? This was a guy that had unlimited cute and sexy women in his teen years. How was it even remotely possible that he would wind up with this woman? What was the ransom? Mind you, if you stripped Bennie of his good looks then Barbara would be par for the course. But this was not the norm that I had become known to expect.

Unlike Bennie's first wife, Barbara was the spouse abuser in that family. My nephew told me of instances in which Bennie had to seek shelter due to Barbara's corrective actions against him. Personally, I was smart enough not to cross her! She appeared very able to whip asses well outside of her weight class!

Where Is Barbara?

TWO MONTHS LATER I would get a call of desperation from Aunt Kathy! She told me that Bennie was gravely ill. She went on to say that Bennie and his wife had been fighting. She then said that she feared that Barbara had poisoned him. When it came to Bennie no one had his best interest except Aunt Kathy. According to her, someone was always doing something to Bennie. Nothing was ever his fault. Bennie's only son looks exactly like him yet Aunt Kathy had no love for him because he wasn't "the real McCoy." She had no respect for the dynamics of the father supporting his children either. She told me that Bennie would go to work with a sandwich and when he returned home he couldn't find a sandwich.

Aunt Kathy said that Bennie was fading fast and I should come right away. I had been taken in by Aunt Kathy's assumptions before; but I felt I should take no chances on this guy's life. He was my brother. I had lost my closest brother to a murder just a year prior so I would be mentally wise to do what I could to help Bennie.

I asked Aunt Kathy, "Who is going to look after Bennie's four little girls?"

She told me, "Barbara will take care of the Qwins." I was somewhat tickled with her "twin" enunciation but I understood the urgency. I didn't dare repeat that Bennie and Barbara actually had four daughters.

I told my wife about Bennie's illness and took off from work. I drove 160 miles from Memphis to Columbus to pick up my brother. Aunt Kathy instructed me to take Bennie to the Veterans' Administration

56

Hospital in Jackson, Mississippi.

This was all too familiar. I had spent time with Bennie at this same hospital in the fall of 1985. Back then, prior to my entry into Jackson State University, Bennie came home drunk and started a fight with Carl. I tried to stay out of it until Bennie grabbed an object and threw it at Carl. As I rushed Bennie, he tried to run out of the apartment and fell over the railing, landing one floor below. As I approached he was lying unconscious. I placed him in my car, rushed him to the local hospital, and got him signed in. Then I headed off to college 150 miles away.

A day later I was told that Bennie was sent to the VA hospital in Jackson, Mississippi due to swelling on the brain. It was as if destruction was following me! I left the school immediately. When I got to the hospital Bennie was sitting up in bed staring straight ahead in a daze. He just looked lost in the head. He didn't even recognize me. He was slurring all of his words. Tears were building and I was deeply afraid I was going to lose him. I had to step away to try to gather myself.

I started walking all about that massive hospital. I walked past room after room. I would read the hospital history out in the lobby. I entered some areas in which I didn't belong. I ended up on a floor where they treated mental disorders. I came upon an orderly by the name of Renae. She was surprised to see me but she welcomed my company. After telling me about herself she told me about her patients.

There was Case Number 1: Harry. He had been in the hospital for about a year. He had a fetish for grooming. This guy was immaculate. His arms, his beard, and his head were teased neatly into place like a mannequin. He even showed his toes and chest; However, Renae stopped him from dropping his pants! I was relieved that she did. Harry then looked at me, spoke, and offered to cut my hair. I politely declined. So he moved on and began harassing his fellow patients.

Case Number 2: Dontae. He was a mentally challenged man that was sexually abused for most of his life. He was about twenty-eight years old, yet he preferred to be regarded as a gay toddler! I couldn't imagine such a thing, but that was Donte's self description. He treated Renae like a mother or a teacher. In the time I was there, Dontae had been pranked by another orderly named James. James had sarcastically told Dontae that he should act his age. Dontae ran up to Renae demanding that she set James straight!

Renae asked, "Dontae, what's wrong, honey?"

Dontae replied, "James told me to act like an ADULT but please tell him that I am a CHILD!" Renae looked at James with tongue-in-cheek and said, "James, Dontae is our CHILD. So leave him alone!"

Dontae stuck out his tongue in the direction of James then off he went to join his friends.

Then there was Case Number 3: Curtis Smoke. He got the name "Smoke" because he would smoke anything that he got his hands on. It didn't matter if it was cigarettes, joints, crack, meth, or paper. He would inhale it if it would burn.

Curtis Smoke didn't care for Renae. Not in the least little bit. So the workers would keep Curtis Smoke separated from Renae as much as possible. However, Renae was having too much fun introducing me to her patients. When she took me over to meet Curtis Smoke, she asked him, "Curtis, why don't you like me?"

Curtis Smoke looked Renae up and down then said,"I only need to look at a woman twice to tell if she is a whore; And Renae, you are a whore!"

That was the laugh that I badly needed. I thanked Renae. I said goodbye to her associates and her patients. Then I returned to Bennie's room. He was apparently making a speedy recovery which allowed me to set my attention back on school.

Now it was 1997 and I was heading back to a familiar place. I wasted no time and got on the road to Jackson, Mississippi. Bennie was very weak. He spent most of the drive in and out of sleep. I got to the hospital on a Saturday afternoon. I was told that they were not seeing any more patients. I pleaded with a doctor to see him. The doctor relented and took Bennie in. About an hour later I was told that Bennie had the flu. I was relieved but I was furious as well. I was pulled out of work. I was taken away from family. I was using my own money for something that could have been handled in Columbus. Oh well, I guess I got a chance to spend some time with my brother and a chance to look for Renae. Surprisingly, she had gotten married and moved on. At least Curtis Smoke didn't taint that relationship!

After treatment Bennie was getting stronger by the hour. It was still Saturday. He started to talk as we got closer to Columbus. He told me that Barbara had probably left for "the Club." I was appalled by the conversation but I figured, "Go ahead and enlighten me to your world."

He came off as if he was either being left out or she was not responsible enough to stay home with their kids! I really couldn't tell which was which. Before I could find out, we were arriving at his home. It was around 7:00 p.m. I stayed in the car as he went inside. Just as he predicted Barbara wasn't there and the kids aged three through nine were all alone. I told him not to worry and to focus on the kids. I went on to say, "If you hear of any Big Foot sightings, you will know where to look for Barbara." Then I headed back to Memphis.

Brotherly Love

IN MAY 1999 I got a wild hair to go to Shreveport, Louisiana with my family to visit my Uncle Dan and his daughters for the Memorial Day weekend. I had no relationship with a male relative so I figured I would try to bond with this uncle. I got to know my dad in 1981, which drove my Aunt Kathy bat crazy! The thought of her not being the center of my world infuriated her.

The fact that my dad could be the equalizer for me versus what she had been to Bennie was intimidating. Yet my relationship with my dad was nowhere near what she had feared. Plus, I was an adult. I was controlling my own destiny. My interactions with Dad was somewhere between an interrogation and a duty. It just wasn't a natural connection. Aunt Kathy got wind of my plans and asked me to include her in our trip. Like a fool I agreed.

As I journeyed toward Shreveport it was touch and go from the start. My Aunt Kathy didn't really know my wife nor my daughter, yet she was trying to control my kid. My bratty daughter was always allowed to get junk food whenever or wherever I would stop. While I was in the restroom Aunt Kathy wouldn't allow my daughter to get any items to which she was accustomed. Of course, my little girl was upset and the wife was on edge from that point on.

I made room reservations with the intent of staying at the Court-Hall Hotel for the complete weekend. Aunt Kathy was desiring to stay with Uncle Dan. I knew then that trouble was lurking on the horizon. When we got to Shreveport on Friday evening, there was no Welcome Wagon or relatives to be found. Yet, we were ok. The pool was great.

The accommodations were nice. It still wasn't good enough for Aunt Kathy. After a couple of unanswered calls I gave up and left the search to Aunt Kathy. Midday Saturday contact and connections were made so we headed over to Uncle Dan's place. His residence was a small home that was made for just one or two persons. All of Uncle Dan's children had moved out. Once inside the house I couldn't help but notice a lock and chain was wrapped tightly around the refrigerator. Strange, I thought. It was the elephant in the room! I kept staring at this refrigerator and scratching my head as to WHY. This man lived alone! What was he protecting? And from whom?

I spent that day trying to engage Uncle Dan but he was evasive and constantly moving about. He would top up his cup of whiskey from time to time but he wasn't making himself available. I had been around the cousins a few times before so those moments were strictly for Uncle Dan and me. After chasing him around for about three hours I blurted out "Hey Uncle, talk to me!"

He turned to me with a sheepish grin and said, "I know what you want."

I was then thinking, "OK, let's see what that produces."

Uncle Dan brought out a picture of himself when he was around thirty years of age with a gun pointed directly at the photographer. I smiled and said, "Cool," but inside I was churning. I honestly found the picture quite disturbing. I told my wife that anyone who takes a picture with their gun will actually use that gun without hesitation!

As we retired back to our hotel I could see that Aunt Kathy was uneasy about something. Turns out she wanted us to stay with Uncle Dan. I wasn't restricting her so I didn't understand her anger. But staying with Uncle Dan was not my intention. Our hotel stay was covered for the entire weekend.

I was awakened on Sunday morning by Aunt Kathy frantically telling me that we should go to Uncle Dan's place. She was speaking at such a rate that I had to slow her down in order to understand her. She was saying, "I spoke to Dan and he said that we could all stay with him. Just throw everything in the car and let's go."

You would have thought that we were being chased by the mob or Uncle Dan was giving away big money! I had to think fast in order to overcome her insane notion of my family sleeping at Uncle Dan's place. I just didn't feel good about him! I told Aunt Kathy that we had made additional plans to meet our college friends at the Court-Hall Hotel. No, it didn't set well, but Aunt Kathy had gotten what she wanted, which was a chance to be with her brother. However, she was upset that we didn't join her.

The cousins invited all of us to their church. I have to admit I gave Aunt Kathy far too much credit. I was her fool once, twice, three, and maybe 1000 times more than I should have been!

During church service the pastor asked the visitors to stand and introduce themselves. Aunt Kathy not only told about herself but also about the preacher of her church back in Columbus, Mississippi. She didn't just stop there! She told how long he had pastored at Zion Union Mission Baptist Church! She told of his travels and the places where he'd been as a guest minister! She must have talked for ten minutes non-stop.

After the recognition of the visitors Aunt Kathy proceeded to show the choir how to perform the song "Leaning On the Everlasting Arms." Then, apparently, she felt disrespected and not received as warmly as she had hoped. At that point she took over that church!

I sheepishly tried to blend in as an ordinary member as Aunt Kathy mocked the church and ordered parishioners around. She kept poking me in the side to keep me keenly focused on her antics as she sang her own rendition! While she sang she stopped momentarily to criticize the members and their progression of service. She belted out the opening verse before the choir had a chance to gather themselves: "What a fellowship, What a joy divine--these people can't sing..."

Then it was, "Look at those bad azz kids!" She kept going back to pick up the lyrics "Safe and Secure from all alarms..." Then it was, "None of these bastards are singing," as she rambled on with another verse "Oh, how sweet to walk in this pilgrim way..." She then said, "Just a bunch of Asses, Asses, Asses in here!" Finally, she finished with a final "Leaning on the Ever Everlasting Armmmms!"

Obviously, there was no place to for me to hide! Next, Aunt Kathy stared me in the face eyeball to eyeball and tore into another song, even though the church tried to move on to the next stage of their program.

It was suddenly her singing "I Love the Lord; He Heard My Cries..." This time she went completely solo. She continued to sing it all by herself while many in the congregation looked on in disgust! I had no choice at that point. Either I escort her out of the church or join in to deflect this ongoing circus. I needed to act and act fast! Being intimidated by her wrath if I dared to remove her, I decided to grab my book of hymns and just sing along! I even attempted to leap a verse ahead of her so as to rush the end of our debacle. "Long as I live, when troubles rise, I'll hasten to your throne..." I sang it loud and I sang it forcefully! But I only made it worse. Aunt Kathy kept singing every verse behind my verses. We ended up doing a duet from hell! We sounded like the breaking of dishes in a quiet restaurant. At the close of service I noticed that no one said, "We hope you all come back again" but Aunt Kathy left with a look of indignation that said, "I showed them!"

Understandably, I got no smiles on the way out either.

We all gathered at a local cafeteria for Sunday dinner. The cousins were adamant that Uncle Dan would not show up because he didn't eat out in public places. However, Uncle Dan arrived, then started to pace back and forth on the outside of the restaurant. Aunt Kathy then stated, "Dan will come inside because he knows I'm in here!"

As predicted, Uncle Dan moseyed in and took a seat right next to Aunt Kathy. Uncle Dan was around sixty years old. Out of nowhere, big sister Aunt Kathy proceeded to feed Uncle Dan spoon by spoon. I looked at my wife with my jaw hanging down to my knees! You could have driven a semi trailer through my pie hole. The site of my aunt and uncle playing feed the baby at their age must have dislocated my upper and lower jaw. I just couldn't imagine my sister feeding me, even if I was immobile.

Real Ice

IT WAS NOW Memorial Day. All the cousins and my family gathered at Uncle Dan's house for the first and only time that weekend. Aunt Kathy was showing major attitude toward us for not staying overnight at Uncle Dan's home. I was keeping my distance from her as well.

Since it was a holiday, I took it upon myself to buy barbecue dinners for all of the relatives in attendance. I personally asked Uncle Dan for his order. He emphatically stated that he was ok. I then went deeper into details offering a list of bottled waters. He cut me off. "o!

"Soda pops?"

He stated No!

"BBQ sandwiches?

"No," he said!

" Cigarettes?"

Another No!

And finally, "Whiskey?"

He gave another resounding No!

He said, "Son, I'm ok!" So off I headed to get the meals. After I returned and gave out the food I entered the kitchen where my wife was preparing the sodas. I saw my uncle bumping and shoving the refrigerator as if he had secretly stuffed an entire hog into his ice box. He placed the lock and chain firmly back around his private frig. I looked toward my wife and she had a troubled expression on her face. I asked her what was going on and she told me that Uncle Dan had taken up everyone's ice. I was thrown off.

I approached Uncle Dan and asked, "Why did you take away our ice?"

He responded with a raspy growl, "I had ice, you didn't ask me if I had ice!"

So here was my run down! I offered bottled water, sodas, BBQ sandwiches, cigarettes, and even whiskey. As dumbfounded as I appeared, I guess it was silly of me to not mention "Ice"! Nonetheless, he wasn't making an effort to share "his ice." He actually locked up my store bought ice in protest! I thought I gave him every opportunity to place an order or to join in the preparations. It appeared that he wanted to feel needed by giving his ice for the sodas! Apparently, we hurt his feelings by using "outside ice."

It was getting dark so we started back to Columbus. Plus, I had had enough of Aunt Kathy's attitude. I was jamming the gas pedal because I wanted to get her home as soon as possible. As I entered The Natchez Trace parkway Aunt Kathy suggested that I should slow down for fear of getting a traffic ticket. I tried to assure her that I had driven on that highway many times before and I was well aware of the times the patrolmen went in for the evening. She then told me, "The patrol cars may be off the road but the Rangers may be out there on a horse!" It took every ounce of my patience to keep from telling her, "Just sit back and ride!"

I looked at Dylan and he looked back at me with a confused expression. Then he bellowed out a laugh! I laughed along with him. We both had a drink. Then the talks went on.

Aunt Kathy Forecasts Her Stroke

UNCLE DAN PASSED in 2012 from a failed heart operation in Houston, Texas. His kids had spent their summers in Crawford which was thirty miles south of Columbus with the grandparents of their mom. When Uncle Dan picked them up from their vacations he would stop in Columbus to visit his sister, Aunt Kathy, but not my mom. I only saw those cousins once in my childhood because they would stay at Aunt Kathy's place. Carl and me were never invited over to greet our relatives from Louisiana. Strangely, Bennie would be invited. He was a jewel to Uncle Dan as well. Those cousins' roots were with the grandparents and not Aunt Kathy or my mom. Right after Uncle Dan's death Aunt Kathy coerced the cousins into having their dad's funeral in Columbus. That was unusual because those ladies hardly knew us or cared for Aunt Kathy!

Aunt Kathy's second career was embalming the dead at a local funeral parlor. She would eerily say that everybody was a potential customer. My cousins' mom preceded Uncle Dan in death in 2010. Aunt Kathy was badly hurt because Uncle Dan and the cousins didn't give her the business of preparing her sister-in-law for burial. Personally, I thought that was way too close for comfort.

In any case, the memorial for Uncle Dan continued as planned in Columbus at Aunt Kathy's church. I drove from Houston the morning of the service for support and final respect. Aunt Kathy had been involved with the arrangements of her brother as much as the cousins. And of course I suppose she should have had a hand in that event since it was her demand that the funeral be held at her doorstep. Aunt

Kathy found something in the obituary that wasn't worded the way she wanted it and she just shut down only hours before the service. As the cousins tried to placate her she screamed "I am having a stroke!" Then she fainted.

They rushed her to the emergency room, then called me with these shameful details while I was still on the way to Columbus. I told them, "No one can forecast a stroke! Maybe a heart attack but not a stroke."

In other words she was faking it! I got to Columbus with enough time to check on Aunt Kathy. She had been released from the hospital. She asked me to pick up some Cold medicine and grocery items. She said nothing about her illness. Yet she still refused to show at the funeral of her most beloved sibling. I guess she showed them!

Roll Call!

DYLAN AGAIN TRANSPORTED me back to the Afghan situation. The nurse was examining me from head to toe. As she combed through my hair, she was clearing dust, glass, and chips of paint. She asked if I was feeling pain in any other places that were not visible. I told her about the blood spot on my pants. She asked me to stand up and undress so she could view my cut. I stepped down off the table and turned toward the wall while dropping my pants about knee high! The room suddenly filled with catcalls and "Yeah, oh Yeah!" remarks. We all laughed as the doctor continued to evaluate my injury. The laughter was a much-needed relief for all of us. Prior to that, everyone was in a catatonic state! No one was talking to anybody and it was an eerie feeling! I saw people do a lot of unusual things. Some were attempting to go back to their demolished rooms for rest and relaxation. People were looking for car keys to vehicles that were destroyed. Others were talking to themselves. And many were just staring and not responding to any questions. I felt so lucky to be alive. But it was like being human amongst zombies.

Yet there was also no structure or organization involved. The camp contingency plans had literally gone up in smoke!

Out of nowhere, Hayward, one of the survivors, decided to do a head count. Everyone was accounted for except two persons. Hayward started gathering volunteers to look for the missing. I honestly didn't want to participate. I had experienced enough terror just to get to where I was, but I couldn't leave coworkers out in the danger without at least making a token attempt to help them.

I asked the nurse about my leg? She said that I would need stitches right away. I said, "Ok, but hurry so I can join the search team."

She gave me a local anesthesia for the pain. Then she pulled out a sewing kit that looked something like fishing gear. And just like that I was back in my childhood!

The School Years:
The Six-Year-Old Flirt

PRESCHOOL WAS A two-week orientation in the middle of summer for kids that were entering the first grade. I was six years old and I couldn't wait to get there. For three years, I had watched Bennie prepare for school. He would leave home with a smile, minus any books or work utensils. He would return home with an even bigger smile, along with borrowed paper, borrowed pencils, and other kids' work assignments.

I got the impression that school was such a joyous place. The kids would yell his name in the streets. However, no one was calling out to me! Bennie was making friends beyond his brothers. Of course, Aunt Kathy had sinful labels for each and every kid that tried to befriend her Bennie.

I wanted to go the fun place. I wanted friends too. But I knew to hide them from Aunt Kathy. I would interrogate Bennie each and every day. I wanted to know more and more about school. I wanted to know about the teachers, the students, his friends, and finally the girls. Bennie didn't offer many details about the teachers. He knew even less about being a student! He was very protective of his friends. In other words they were not to be my friends. Yet, he didn't mind talking about the girls. Even at the age of nine he talked about a lot of pretty girls that he knew! I was spellbound. I wanted to meet pretty girls just like my big brother! I was deeply amazed but what do I do? What do I say? I was just psyched by the unknown. I kept pestering

Bennie for details. I told him that he had to tell me what to do! I didn't want to look bad.

Suddenly, he said, "You can't be like me. I'm Bennie!"

I didn't know what that meant but I would soon find out. After days of my being a nuisance, Bennie gave in and gave me pointers of how to handle the girls. He told me, "As you walk past the girls, just tip your hat and smile!"

Like a champ I committed that nugget to my social repertoire. The day of school I left home with glee and determination. I had a pep in my step and a song in my heart. I was on my way to class when I quickly came upon a set of female twins named Mary and Martha who were slowly walking in my direction. They had to be about nine years of age and, unlike myself, attending summer school. They were all of 5 feet 9 inches tall whereas I was only 4 feet 10 inches. Their height didn't matter. I saw them as two full glasses of lemonade!

Since it was the dead of summer I was wearing a cap to shield my face from the Mississippi sun. As I approached the twins I smiled, I tipped my hat, then I continued on my way. I had done the "big move" just like Bennie had instructed. I had a smile from jawline to jawline! I was so full of myself! Out of nowhere one of the girls grabbed my cap, while the other twin delivered a blow to my head! I had been slapped silly! I couldn't even feel my tongue She actually slapped the taste right out of my mouth! I spun around to face my bullies. The twins had become triplets. I couldn't remember ever trying to drink three glasses of anything. This wouldn't be the day to try either! The twins stared at me. One asked, "Who the hell do you think you are?"

The third girl apparently disappeared. I shrugged my shoulders in fear, staring back at the twins. They gave me back my cap and told me to get lost. I didn't challenge those instructions. So much for Bennie's advice! I needed to create my own playbook.

The Little Rattler

THE GIRLS AT school hated me with a passion. I'm sure I presented a mental conflict for them. I was a semi-handsome kid with a shameful connection with "the Crazy Lady that Rides a Bike." So they would rather beat me up than try to be my friend. In the third grade there was this cute girl named Stephanie that all the boys admired. She was the smallest and prettiest thing in the class. But she was as mean as a rattlesnake. Funny how no one else thought that except me! She was the teacher's pet and the doll of the class. She got away with every-thing. She would frame me just for laughs and her own wickedness! Once she threw a brick at me in the middle of the classroom. She even got away with it! I caught her rage and her fury every weekday from 8:00 a.m. to 4:00 p.m. Some days I would even catch her venom on the way home! She would have her rattler friends, primarily girls, antagonizing me all the way to my doorstep. She was just as cunning as she was cute. Every so often I would catch a blow in the back or a shove to the head from one of her friends because Stephanie kept me distracted in a fight!

My brother, Bennie, thought I had the juice since Stephanie and her serpents would be seen following me home! He was too dense to notice that my arrival wasn't with the most positive fanfare! I would be missing a shirt, or a shoe, or a couple of books because I had to take on Stephanie and her Vipers just to get to the door.

I don't remember tipping my hat to her, or smiling at her, or saying anything out of place to her, yet she had it in for me! It never failed. If the teacher left the room all the students would move their desks just to make room for us to fight. I never fought her hard because I didn't want to hurt her, yet the fights would ensue just about every day. And almost daily I was in trouble for fighting. I could be in the middle of my workbook and suddenly I would hear the screeching of desks moving outwardly. I knew immediately that meant protect yourself and come out swinging.

Stephanie would do things just to prove to me how bad she was! She would grab my test paper, copy my answers, then show me our identical results after being graded.

Our teacher would make us eat all of our lunch items regardless of our appetite. Some kids would ditch the foods they didn't care for. I hated cooked carrots! Stephanie would frequently tell our teacher that I threw out my carrots. I would be forced to eat a second helping while Stephanie and the teacher looked on.

Stephanie had to be stopped! I had to find a way to get her off my back! My hair was about to turn orange from my heavy consumption of cooked carrots. I needed revenge but without beating her up.

I found out that Stephanie really looked forward to Christmas, just like most kids. Everyone was creating their lists for Santa when I brought up the topic of the Big Lie! I opened the conversation by stating that Santa was really our parents and not a fantasy guy with a beard. I even added that only the good kids would get the gifts that Christmas. Stephanie had no father at home just like myself! I made sure to talk in Stephanie's direction as we engaged one another. Stephanie knew that she had been a rotten person for all of that year! Her tears flowed for fear of being left out by Santa Claus! Miraculously, my plan did work. Stephanie never threw any more poison my way after that. Happily, she moved away before the fourth grade. But she was awfully cute—just too bad about the hateful venom!

Dylan murmured, "You started young, huh?" I grinned at him and I kept talking.

Beat His Marbled Ass

ONE OF THE cheapest games we played was shooting marbles. All the stores sold them. They would even sell marbles individually. There was the Big Mama, an oversized marble. That one was an anomaly. No one really wanted it but we all had one. There were the Bumble Bees and the Cat eyes. Mostly everyone chased after the Bumble Bees. I had very little entertainment in the house and no books to read so I practiced shooting marble from sunrise to sunset. I got to be pretty good. I was acquiring quite a collection of the other kids' marbles. Our elementary was divided into two sections. The lower level (grades one through three) and the upper level (grades four through six). The lower level was barred from playing at the upper level at all times. That restriction was for me as well. But I was beating all the kids at the lower so profoundly that my only competition was with the bigger boys at the upper level. I was only a second grader yet I got some respect when it came to that game.

Bennie and me got to school very early one morning with nothing to do before class. As I walked into my classroom I could hear the kids at the upper level playing marbles. Yes!, I thought. Another chance to take those suckers down. Then I realized that I had left my marble bag at home. I knew I couldn't borrow any from the guys because I wasn't well liked enough for that. I would sneak and play with them all the time. Fortunately, I was never caught! But those guys hated losing to a 2nd grader. But foolishly, their pride wouldn't allow them to stop playing against me!

I needed just a few marbles to get into the game. There was a fish tank in the classroom across from my homeroom and marbles were in this tank. So I walked in while thinking that no one would see me. I rolled up my sleeves and took about four marbles. I went up to the restricted end and beat those guys senseless. As I walked back to class, I probably had about forty new marbles for my collection. I was happy. I was whistling and walking with sheer joy in my heart. It was 8:00 a.m. Time for class but no one was there. My class was gathered in the room from which I stole the marbles.

The year was 1967 and the schools in Mississippi were still segregated. All the teachers were African American and all the students were African American. Most of the kids, including myself, were afraid of those teachers. They used a form of discipline that was most definitely child abuse. However, I was a bored and mischievous kid. Not that I was seeking attention, but school wasn't much of a challenge at that time so I wandered into many other areas.

This 2nd grade class was taught by Mrs. Dorthy. She was about 6 feet 2 inches tall while tipping the scales at about 200 pounds. No one, and I mean no one, dared to mess with Mrs. Dorthy.

As I peered into her classroom she was ripping Bennie a new one! He was hanging tough but tears were forming. As I caught his eyes I spoke with my lips "PLEASE DON'T TELL! Oh GOD, PLEASE DON'T TELL!"

Next up was a kid named Sonny Lincoln. Sonny was known as the disobedient kid of the second grade. Someone had fingered Bennie and him for taking the marbles out of the fish tank. There I was standing and shaking like a leaf, watching this slaughter of Bennie while knowing full well that Sonny was going to be next unless something earth-shattering took place. I was not going to trade places with Sonny! I was not going to come clean after seeing what Mrs. Dorthy had delivered to Bennie!

Sonny knew he was on the chopping block long before Mrs. Dorthy finished with my brother. As a matter of fact he was already crying, pleading, and imploring for someone to believe his innocence! As Mrs. Dorthy grabbed Sonny and started into him, he was crashing to the floor and swaying left and right. He kept scooting behind her as she tried to whip him! He was screaming, "It wasn't me! It wasn't me, Mrs. Dorthy!"

His outcries gained no merit, but suddenly Mrs. Dorthy lost her grip on Sonny's hand! He quickly headed for the door. Mrs. Dorthy rebounded and shut the door on Sonny's leg which was all that was left inside the doorway. Sonny was shouting and digging with the one foot that was trapped. "Oh Lord, Oh Lord!" he squealed. Out of something like mercy Mrs. Dorthy suddenly let up! She opened the door. Sonny shot out of the school building and was racing toward home. Mrs. Dorthy went out, got in her car, and brought Sonny back to school. She would then finish beating the sense out of him. Hell, yes, I quit playing marbles at school.

Mr. Tough:

IN THE 4TH grade I started to hit my academic stride once again. I'm sure it was because I thought the teacher was Hot! Otherwise, I would have stayed in the middle of the pack as usual. Ms. King was tall, shapely, cute, and energetic, with an engaging personality. She put the clamps on my participation because I was answering far more than my share of questions. I felt my classmates were too slow and too unknowledgeable.

I came up with another ploy for attention. I would clear my throat as if to say, "I'm your man!"

Ms. King would tease me, asking, "Why are you clearing your throat, young man?"

I told her that it was because "I was tough," even though I knew I was flirting with her. "Tough" became Ms. King's nickname for me during the 4th grade. When none of the kids had the answers she would turn to "Tough." As I gave the correct answers I'd smile and tugged on my shirt collar. That was way too much arrogance for my classmates, so the fights and name calling ensued! I got into fights before school, at recess, at lunch, and on the way home. My peers were determined to find out just how tough I really was. It became obvious that they were even tagging one another into the fights. I was a one man gang against the Southside Crew. I have to admit I had a shameful win/loss record. No one was willing to tag in on my behalf. I took a lot of bumps and blows to the head just to be out front for the teacher. Please no more questions for me.

What Is Love?

OUR SCHOOL INTEGRATED when I entered the 5th grade (1970). The White kids were bused to our school. Most of them were the Palmer Home (orphanage) kids. That was a new experience to all involved. There would be fights nearly every day. To be honest we didn't know why we were fighting because most had no interaction with White people at all! As the year progressed we started to settle down and get along with one another. Due to me being constantly ridiculed and attacked, I had a skill for watching and observing people. I was amazed how the Palmer Home kids had a hierarchy and a brotherhood even though they were not related. They were kids without parents but they supported each other like blood relatives. Even though I was never part of the fighting bunch, they were very difficult to get to know. It could have been their new atmosphere. Or it could have been their "Us against the world" mentality.

We moved to the "RED LINE" shotgun houses around 1968. This community was across from Friendship Confederate Cemetery. Not very far from our community was an apartment complex that had only White residents. One of my new classmates named Nate lived in that complex. His mom would drop him off at school every day. I would observe Nate each and every day as he said goodbye to his mother. He kissed her before he headed off to class. Those kisses blew our minds—especially me. I wasn't used to that type of fondness between a parent and a child. Plus, we kinda thought he was too old for that stuff! Nonetheless, I was spellbound by their public display of affection!

Nate was the new kid. He started showing signs of becoming "the

Smart GUY." I only allowed select kids to take that title. Even though others scored better than I did, I was never intimidated by their performances. Yet, Nate was different. He was a loner much like myself and he was eating school up! I was definitely in awe and jealous to boot. Long story short I got into a disagreement with Nate and I threatened to beat him up after school. Nate was probably the smallest male in the 5th grade. I figured I would wolf at him and he would cower down out of fear.

The venue was set. After school everyone knew there was going to be a fight at the flagpole between the two geeky kids. I would get to the site first. I had people holding my books. Like a scene from a Western movie that scrawny pale White kid showed up prepared to fight. I was flabbergasted! He wasn't going to back down. I looked Nate in the face and said, "Man, I am not going to fight you. If you are bold enough to show up here while surrounded by African American kids then you definitely have my respect."

Who knows? Nate may have mopped the streets with me. I wouldn't recommend anyone to do what Nate did but I was impressed. Believe it or not, I walked Nate home. We became the best of buds from that point until his mom met "the Crazy Lady that Rides a Bike."

Nate and I would compare our homework. I even had to up my academic game because of Nate. I had to show him that I was the "Silent Champ."

His mom would invite me over quite often to play with him. She would even ask me to stay for dinner but I never accepted. Unexpectedly, Nate and his mom dropped by to meet my mom. That surprise went very badly! Mom cursed and shouted at them for no reason whatsoever. I was so embarrassed. I could only look at my mom in anger and disgust! Of course, she didn't care! I had no clue where her rage came from. But honestly she was always looking for a confrontation. Nate and I would never hang out again. We would drift apart even at school. It wasn't long before Nate and his mom moved away.

When Fire Is Your Friend

BEING NOBODY WITH no connections kept me at the back of the class in school and in life. I was the person about which almost everyone could say, "At least I am better than that guy!" I became so accustomed to it that I expected everything coming my way to be "hand-me-downs", or "throw-aways." Yet I learned to be quite creative making crap look fashionable.

As I reached the 7th grade my day to day attire was fading badly. There was no masking it either. One day after school I was out playing sandlot football in my school clothes when Sonny Lincoln asked me if I wore those same clothes to school. I didn't hesitate. "Yes", I said. The pants I was wearing were clearly too small. The gym shoes were busted and the cheapest brand possible. The shoes were called "Catfish" or "Cats" for short. No one wanted to be caught dead in a pair of "CATS" as a teenager.

Sonny had quit school about two years prior. I couldn't help but think, "Wow, he is well dressed yet he has no school to attend!" Going forward, that moment created my love for fashion. Yet there was nothing I could do about it. No money was no money! I had quit working months earlier so I had no job to help me procure the clothing that I needed.

At that time we were living in a one bedroom shack with a huge fireplace. There was nothing romantic about the fireplace because we needed it for warmth throughout the day and throughout the night. So I was constantly fetching wood in cold and sometimes in dark conditions.

Mom was just a very careless and irresponsible person. If she was having one of her rants or episodes then she would leave the house without putting out the fire.

I got called to the school office in the winter of the 7th grade. My mind was racing! I was thinking mom had stopped by to embarrass me. She had done it so many times before. But there was no mom. So, what could it be? The counselor told me that our house had burned down. I looked at her and said, "Ok, thanks."

Normally kids would become hysterical and dissolve in tears due to their sudden loss. The counselor was somewhat shocked at my response. So she repeated it to make sure I heard her correctly. I told her once again "Yes, I do understand you." Yet I was thinking that we didn't lose much. I knew it was a blessing but I wasn't sure to what extent.

My 6th grade teacher, Mrs. Cousins, elevated me to being her star student. She saw through my lackadaisical attitude. She knew how to pull the best out of me. She had a warmth and sense of encouragement that stayed with you long after class was over!

She impressed me far more than she would ever know. However, I thought I was just one of many students that admired her.

Mrs. Cousins' husband was a pilot at the Columbus Air Force Base. He would die in a plane crash after I left elementary school. I was so saddened for her loss because she was such a wonderful person. I felt as if I had lost someone as well!

Anyway after the house fire I was out of school for about two days. We were staying with Aunt Kathy until Mom found another shack. Out of thin air this White lady comes to the Aunt Kathy's house to check on me. I was nearly moved to tears! I was so impressed that an ex-teacher would go to such an extent to reach out to me. It was Mrs. Cousins. I was so overjoyed to see her. I wanted to hug her and ask if she was ok, being that she lost her husband. Yet I never said a word. I knew not to upstage Aunt Kathy with my conversation, but it felt so darn good to see her again!

I will forever regret not speaking up but her presence spoke to my soul! She would soon move back to Massachusetts and I would never see her again!

During my time away from school, donations would begin coming in. I received clothing from Goodwill and the Salvation Army that made me a totally new guy. I used my creativity to make everything look like new. I was so happy because suddenly I could fit in! As it turned out the kids hated me for my abrupt modifications! They were so content and so used to me being "The bum across the room." They were completely threatened and disgusted by my new look. It was time to put me back in my place. So day after day I was attacked as the Salvation Army guy. Plus, being "the kid whose mom rides a bike" was always a solid hit.

The Fantasies That I Knew!
A Laugh for All Seasons

THERE WAS NEVER anything great about the holidays except time away from school. Yes, I would get that warm fuzzy feeling due to the seasons or the displays but that was where it ended. For me there was nothing else to look forward to. No aroma of baked cakes or baked pies in the air. No visions of turkey, chicken, or glazed hams calling your name. Mom didn't cook or delve into such preparations. Her go-to was the Salvation Army or whatever her employers gave her. I resented that frame of mind! Yes, I ate the food that she was lucky enough to receive but the thought that other people or organizations controlled my happiness bothered me.

I remember specifically asking her one Christmas "Where are our gifts?" and she told me "You can have an orange."

Even the fruit most likely came from the Salvation Army or a church donation. That became such a joke for Carl and me. The lead-in would be, "Carl, I have your Christmas gift" while I was hiding a piece of fruit behind my back! His response would be something like, "Yeah, right." Then I would offer him a gift-wrapped orange or a gift-wrapped apple! Of course, he would try to pull that same trick on me at a later time.

Each year there would be a campaign on the local TV station to get kids to write to Santa Claus. I jumped on it like a kid possessed. I would even buy my own stamps and envelopes. Each year I got my letter (or letters in case the elves misplaced the original one) in earlier than the year before. On Christmas Eve I followed all of the rituals of milk and cookies and getting to bed early. On Christmas Day I was stunned and brokenhearted that Santa missed our house. I didn't know if I was a bad kid, or he was afraid of Mom or, he just ran short of gifts! Like all kids at Christmas I was definitely in denial about being a "bad kid."

I would tell myself that next year would be the "Big One" for me and Santa would make up for years past.

In the meantime I would see a parade of kids with new toys and new bicycles with big smiles that would melt the toughest Grinch. I simply couldn't wait for the holidays to be over.

No doubt we were THE TROUBLED kids from time to time. I would say it was because of a lack of discipline, a lack of respect, and a lack of training. Mom didn't teach us nor push us to be decent kids so we got into whatever dared to gain our interest. This was more so me than anyone else. I was just curious, courageous, and even diabolical at times. If Mom disciplined us then it was certainly abuse to the umpteenth degree. She would smash us (Carl and me) with shoes, spoons, and anything she could get her hands on. Of course, Bennie was exempt from that type of punishment!

There was a public service ad on television in the early '70s stating "It shouldn't hurt to be a Child." Carl and me grew closer due to our humor and our fights. So whenever the other one got SMASHED by Mom we would tease each other with the slogan, "It SHOULDN'T HURT TO BE A CHILD." Within seconds it would be on! We would fight until we were both laughing! We were just weird like that.

The Little Wino

MOM WAS CRAZY but she also had a shapely figure. So despite her antics she found men that would come over. Funny how that worked! I didn't respect any of them, nor did Mom make me behave. IF they fell asleep, I was either trying to rob them or I was trying to drive their vehicle. If I was awake then I was keeping them busy! They were constantly trying to locate their wallets or find their car keys. Trust me I would have them both. The men would need a briefing on how to deal with a kid like me. Even though I gave them grief I must have been seeking fatherly attention.

After so many scavenger hunts for personal items, it was time to teach me a lesson. One of her friends gave me a couple shots of wine. He went directly to the emergency section of his orientation. As a five-year-old I was thinking that it was simply good-tasting grape juice. At that age it wouldn't have taken a lot to send me into a tailspin. I must have gulped down about a full cup of the stuff. I would spend the evening stumbling around and throwing up everything I had eaten for the past month! I didn't challenge the guy at all after that.

The smart guys didn't hang around very long with my behavior! Or maybe it was Mom's lack of balance! I wouldn't place a bet either way.

Then there came the drunks. They all had a bigger passion for alcohol—more than anything or anyone else. They all smoked. And none of them had a car. Not having a vehicle cut the issue of dealing with a mischievous kid like me right in half!

There was this guy named "Bo" who actually worked the grounds of the Friendship Cemetery. It took years for me to like him. The fact that he was a Joe Frazier fan and I was a Muhammad Ali fan didn't help his cause. Whenever I saw Bo he was always drunk. I'm sure he was a functional alcoholic even on the job. I never saw him standing without a bottle or a cigarette in his hand. But the more he was around the more I would engage him. He was actually a fairly smart guy. I learned a lot from him. Looking back, he stimulated my mind more than any man I had ever been around.

Finally, there was Ezell. I hated him from the start. He smelled. He was almost always drunk. He smoked. And he lied all the time. There was nothing to like about him. Aunt Kathy would come by and always throw him out. Those were the only times I felt sorry for Ezell. He had to have possessed nerves of steel. Or maybe he was too drunk to even care! He saw Aunt Kathy's 38 special so often that I'm sure that he could describe her gun in great detail. Maybe that was the endearing quality that Mom liked about him. He had to be desperate or off kilter to ignore Aunt Kathy's many threats.

I would hardly say a word to the guy. After I reached the age of twenty-four I came to realize how much of a piss-ant I was when it came to my mom's social life. I decided I would accept Ezell even with his shortcomings.

Ezell would ask me if I had clothes so he could attend church with my mom. "No problem" I said! I had plenty of quality suits that I was no longer wearing. So I had them tailored and shipped to Ezell. He loved me for his new look. We would talk a lot whenever I was home. After he passed away in 2014, I did shed a tear. He had been with mom for nearly thirty years. Not only had Mom lost a friend but so did I!

Bennie in the Remix

THERE WERE THINGS that Bennie did that stayed with me for years upon years. He had to be a runner-up to Mom. He would pack his dirty clothes in a suitcase, then walk to the nearest laundromat just to have them cleaned. It took awhile for people to stop sending him well-wishes in his travels. He never bothered to tell anyone that he was only washing his clothes until they would see his quick return!

Whiskey was the magic bullet to Bennie's super powers. As he got drunker, he would eventually take on the world. He would fight King Kong after he got a drop of liquor. He got to where he would drink more and more, hoping to get even greater super powers. Eventually, he would pass out. He once fell asleep on the corner near Aunt Kathy's house. She was called out to check on him. Aunt Kathy would shake and shake him back to consciousness. Bennie would sit up and profess to be a preacher. Aunt Kathy snapped and slapped Bennie back to sobriety! She wanted no competition for her Pastor Lloyd.

As mentioned earlier, after Bennie was divorced from his first wife, DeAna, he went on to marry Barbara, who beat him like a snare drum. DeAna would get remarried as well. One day Barbara had threatened to put Bennie in check with some "tough love." He would bolt out of the house in an attempt to seek refuge or some whiskey before taking Barbara on. As Bennie retreated he ran into DeAna's husband who happened to be driving nearby. Bennie dashed desperately into his car, narrowly escaping Barbara's hot pursuit! DeAna's husband was 6 feet 5 inches tall and 230 pounds.

Bennie was 5 feet 6 inches tall and 145 pounds. Inside the car with DeAna's husband were Bennie's son and a two-year-old little girl. Bennie would look at the little girl in confusion, then shout at DeAna's husband in disgust, "I know damn well you didn't get DeAna pregnant!" Bennie's refuge was immediately gone, and he was immediately forced out of the car. Plan B would be his only option.

In 1984 I would meet Bennie and Mom at the State prison in Parchman, Mississippi. My brother, Carl, had been assigned there for a murder he committed just a year prior. As I got there, I noticed that Mom had such a downcast look on her face. I was undoubtedly spooked as well. The place was as fortified as any movie I had ever seen. There were men with high powered rifles roaming about and watching each and every move. That place was definitely not a dream tour. I didn't see Bennie initially so I kept searching the parking lot for him. I found him talking with other visitors who had family members in jail as well. The only difference was Bennie was so drunk that he could barely stand. His eyes were watery and blood shot. I was thinking, "Why would he come here in such a condition? What will happen when the officials find out? Will they arrest me as well?"

I lost it and I screamed at Bennie, "Why are you so drunk?"

He just smiled at me and said, "Don't worry, my man!"

His words didn't give me an ounce of comfort at all! I was wrestling with the thought of getting into my car and returning back to Jackson. I couldn't be taken in if I never approached the gate with that idiot. Only because of Mom did I decide to stay, instead of returning to school without even seeing Carl.

I went on to usher Bennie in and out of the prison while hoping to God that no one noticed his drunken state. We got lucky or they just didn't care. On the way out I got a shout out from across the room. Now I was even more uneasy. Who would know me in this prison except my brother Carl! Needless to say, I did know the young man that called out my name. But I wasn't looking for a roommate.

After we exited the prison I knew I had to have a heart to heart talk with Bennie. I told him that if he spends most of his time being drunk, then he would miss some of the important things in life! Bennie replied, "Important things like what?" I gave up and headed back to college.

Money or No Money

I'M SURE EVERYONE in the RED LINE community was on some type of Welfare. We were the poster kids for the program. Most families were usually too embarrassed to admit to receiving any assistance. If you were seen using food stamps (SNAPS) then you would be shamed by those who felt they were better off. Since Mom didn't prepare our meals she would give us those coupons as a means to feed ourselves. Imagine a seven-year-old buying his own breakfast or dinner. I would have chips, candy, cookies, and Cokes day after day. I'm sure my addiction to junk food added to my slow growth. Even still, our connection to food stamps was just another opportunity to humor or humiliate one another. The local stores that accepted those coupons would give you a credit or due bill that actually looked like a sales receipt. That receipt would guarantee your return to the same store.

Bennie and me would convince our younger brother, Carl, that the sales receipt was an actual due bill (or due credit). Honestly, it was most likely one of my sick ideas. We would send Carl shopping, knowing that he would get rejected! To add extra punch, we would tell Carl to pick out something that was a favorite only to him. We knew the outcome long before Carl left the house. Keeping a straight face was our biggest challenge. Once Carl left the house we would be in stitches! The tears and the look on Carl's face after his return was exactly what we had expected. Sadly, his reactions kept motivating us (or me) to keep pulling that stunt on him. Occasionally, we would give him the real "due bill" just to make sure the trick had longevity. It was awfully mean. But I guess you can say we were hazing our younger brother!

"Get Him, Mom"!

AT THE AGE of nine, Carl and me would journey away from home a lot, mainly out of boredom or to find something different to eat like plums, pears, peaches, or watermelons. All of those fruits do grow plentifully in Mississippi. You just have to know where to find them. Carl and I were returning home from one of our outings when his classmate persuaded us to climb the neighbor's pear tree. It didn't take a lot of convincing since she was cute and we were still looking for fruit. Within minutes the homeowner showed up and caught us in his pear tree. He was furious! He forced Carl and me into his truck. He took us around to his friends and his family who took turns cussing and threatening to beat us. I kept my poker face the whole time. That angered them even more. It was obvious that they were trying to scare us to tears. It worked on Carl but not on me. So they kept levying all sorts of attacks at me while hoping I would fold under the insults! Finally, he took us home with the intent to get Mom to whip us. Before he got to our place I did show a slight grin. By then I knew that our nightmare would become his nightmare! When he stopped at our house Carl and me jumped out of the truck and ran inside. We didn't have to say a word. Before he could even present Mom with our transgressions she was cussing, attacking, and throwing things at him and his truck. It was the only time that I was delighted to see Mom go from zero to crazy!

No Starter Pistol

WHENEVER THERE IS a gun in the house, kids will find it like a tornado in a trailor park. Mom bought a 22 pistol which in itself was frightening. Carl and I would play with it when she left for work. I was nine years old and Carl was six. We took the bullets out and practiced aiming it. Strangely, we never fired it or ever got hurt. Carl and I would fight just because he had a smart mouth. After he learned where Mom kept her gun, if I punched him out, he would get it chase after me! Not to be outdone, I had my psychotic moment with Mom's gun. I was out practicing with my marbles when a crowd of teenagers stopped near the house to belittle me, hurling insults about Ms. Liza! Right before I resigned to tears I ran inside to get Mom's gun! Instead of scattering and running away they huddled behind each other. As I was taking aim to scare them I was suddenly attacked from behind. It took about twenty minutes before an older guy was able to disarm me. Shortly thereafter, Aunt Kathy came and took Mom's gun. It was the smartest thing for which I can give Aunt Kathy credit! But like a premonition Carl would shoot and kill a guy in 1983 and serve three years of prison time at Parchman State Prison.

A Bullet Has No Name

AUNT KATHY MAY have taken Mom's pistol but she didn't break her desire to have a gun. Out of nowhere Mom would get a 22 rifle that she kept in the closet. Mom's mental disorder was just pure entertainment for those that knew us. As we fast forward to the next summer, we saw first hand that teenagers were just bold, bored, and completely stupid! After playing outside and exhausting ourselves, Bennie, Carl, and me went in for the evening. Like a moth to a flame the teens followed us, then started throwing rocks against the house. They were trying to draw Mom out for one of her many shows. She would peep out to tease them but mostly she wasn't biting. Now they started dashing to the front door and banging on it. They were desperate for her appearance. It was as if they had paid money for a performance! They wouldn't quit. There were chants of "Liza, Liza, Liza!"

Normally, Mom would have been overjoyed to accept their curtain call but that night she was mostly quiet with a troubling grin. Maybe she had performed her final act for that day or maybe she wanted to lure them into a deeper and darker side! I watched in sudden fright as Mom reached for her rifle. As the teens went to bang on the door one last time Mom fired a shot that ricocheted off the door and struck Bennie in the shoulder like a scene from a firefight! He screamed and I screamed because I thought he was badly hurt! Bennie was rushed to the hospital where it was discovered that the bullet had only broken his skin. Bennie would be ok. The cops came out and took Mom's rifle away! She would never get another gun that I knew of. God was definitely looking out for all the fools involved!

Dylan blurted out, "Wow, Crap!"

I said, "Man, Are you ok?"

He just sat and stared with his arms folded. I then asked if I could go on and he said, "Sure."

I gave Dylan a moment for a cigarette. Then I said, "Ok, here we go" and I pushed onward.

Throwing Piss Out a Window

WE DID HAVE a couple of pets starting with a cat that was killed by stray dogs; then a hen which Bennie chased until it was within our living perimeter; and a dog, Spot, that happened to follow us home. We ended up eating the hen which I felt was an unnecessary sacrifice.

Spot was a puppy when we got him. We pampered him and attempted to train him to be an attack dog. Some of his training did take, even though we had no real knowledge of what we were doing. As the saying goes, Spot was like family. He was very protective if anyone showed aggression toward us. Otherwise, he was a very social animal.

It didn't take long before Spot's training would pay off. Bennie and me were out shooting marbles when Arthur Lewis, one of the community bullies, stopped by to pick a fight with Bennie. Without hesitation, I commanded Spot to attack him. Our dog bit Arthur and ran him off and out of sight. Arthur was a fourteen-year-old thug that didn't take my action lightly. He certainly had revenge in his heart. He sneaked back that night and broke Spot's leg. We couldn't afford a veterinarian so Bennie and I put splints on Spot's leg.

Miraculously, our medical attention did work, even though Spot had a slight limp thereafter. Eventually, Spot would disappear forever. I am willing to bet that Arthur had something to do with that as well. We could not prove what happened to Spot but Arthur was a vicious and heartless bully. My dog was only phase one of his plan. Next, he wanted to get me for sending my dog after him. Little did he know I was thinking about revenge as well! But that's just how bullies are.

They are so zeroed in on their supposed advantage that they fail to think that they can be outsmarted. By observing darkness and sickness for so many years I had learned to see people's flaws. Especially, the idiots!

Our "shot gun shack" stood on blocks about two feet tall. We shared an outside toilet with one of the neighbors. The women and infants would urinate in a pot at night rather than go to those outside toilets. There was no hot water, neither were there showers or bathtubs. My two-year-old brother, Tommy, would use the inside pot during the night.

Arthur had been stalking me and making threats on a daily basis. He would not rest until he beat me up!

I knew not to go outdoors because Arthur would surely catch me and do me in. Lacking patience, Arthur showed up at my bedroom window with anger and contempt. He issued threats of ripping me apart! I told Arthur to standby as I fetched the container full of urine. In the middle of his threats, I dashed him with the pee from the pot.

Arthur began shouting and swearing at such a pitch that he kept all of our neighbors up until the wee hours of the morning. Generally, I would not have cared, but he stayed around for what seemed like forever.

Fearing a beat down, I didn't go outside for weeks. Finally I thought the coast was clear, and I decided to test the waters. Unfortunately, I picked the wrong day! Arthur snuck up from behind and leveled me into submission! But he never bothered me again. I learned nothing from that exchange except to be more cunning and more patient in the future.

I found out from experience that bullies feed off each other, especially if they are related like Arthur, Skullhead Ned, and Teddy Charles. They were also close in age. They fed off the weak like hyenas to road kill. Arthur and Teddy Charles were the toughest but Skullhead Ned was always the instigator. He enjoyed beating the helpless more than did his cousins. If one of them bullied you, then the other two were sure to grab a bite out of your ass as well. Once I fell out with Arthur I knew I was in the spin cycle for ass beatings from Skullhead Ned and Teddy Charles. However, Teddy Charles would leap the chain of fear and bodily harm. I must have been the dead meat that he had badly longed for! Teddy Charles was a year older and was thought to be the fiercest of the three. His mission was to succeed where Arthur had failed. Normally, Skullhead Ned would have gotten his licks in, while leaving Teddy Charles to be the Finisher. Apparently, Teddy Charles didn't want Skullhead Ned to soften me up any further. He must have wanted to clobber me in grand fashion all by himself!

Just like a sequel to a horror movie, Teddy Charles frightened me into taking cover inside the house to avoid an immediate shellacking! There he was at the same bedroom window and with similar threats to beat me into a mud-hole. He was showing such rage and hatred that I feared for my own eventual destruction. I have to admit that I did have second and third thoughts about showering him with pee. But he kept his foot on the gas. His curse words became louder and more degrading. He even went as far as to say that he would kick our door in and beat my mom's ass! That convinced me that he needed a taste of Tommy's Piss. His persistence and utter disdain eliminated any doubts I had of sparing him the same humiliation of his predecessor. Plus, I knew I was on the spit for two additional ass beatings no matter what I did to Teddy Charles. No doubt they were going to take turns getting their hit on my ass like a joint at a hippie convention.

Back in the sixties there was a chemical called lye that Mom used for making soap. Lye would combust like the "Drano" of today. When mixed with water, this agent would bring water to a boil.

While Teddy Charles was barking at me I asked him to stand by as I went to gather Tommy's urine pot. Believe it or not Teddy obliged! I added the lye so as to prevent this guy from giving the same embarrassing showcase that Arthur had given. I eased the pot to the window. Teddy Charles observed my every move except the mixing of the Lye.

Teddy showed no fear or apprehension. He admitted to seeing me dragging the urine to the window. He stood up straight and dared me one last time. Then he lunged at me with all his might! I had been holding the urine pot firmly while waiting for the perfect chance to shower him. Without warning Teddy was in my face,, but I greeted him with a pot full of hot boiling piss! Teddy Charles suddenly screamed and shouted "Oh lord, Oh Lord"!

He then hauled ass toward home but I could still pick up his out-bursts: "Oh Lord, Oh Lord!" The screams became more faint in the distance but I could still hear the sheer terror.

Teddy Charles vacated my window and the Red Line community! I didn't have to worry about him disturbing my neighbors like his blood relative, Arthur Lewis.

Of course I went through the same ritual of staying inside until I thought it safe to go out again. But it's never safe when you commit such a despicable act. Did I know that? Of course I did! But Teddy Charles was so bold that I couldn't resist giving him what he needed. Once again I knew I had to leave the house at some point.

After about three weeks I ventured out to play. In the middle of playing I saw the eyes of my playmate swell as if he had seen a were-wolf behind me. It was horror indeed. It was Teddy Charles and he was raining down blows with anger and fury! Quickly, I covered up in the fetal position. I screamed in pain but also to draw attention for a rescue. Teddy Charles had a terrible speech impediment. As lay on the ground I kept yelling for help while applying for my Oscar of the year! Teddy Charles would make the mistake of lecturing me while I was balled like a turtle. He had a very sloppy stutter. He would say, "You threw wee on me! I washed my pace, I washed my pace, I washed my pace, and it still stunk!" After hearing Teddy Charles I couldn't help but laugh while blowing my Academy Award. Teddy didn't think it was funny! He punched me a few more times, but he never bothered me again after that.

In my head I knew the spit had rotated to Skullhead Ned, as the next thug to get a bite out of my ass! However, he cowered down af-ter finding out about his "Top Dog" Teddy Charles' facial cleanse. He wanted no part of my Trilogy!

I peeked over at Dylan and he had this belly-aching growl while rocking back and forth! I didn't bother to ask if he was ok. His actions said it all. I signaled the staff to get Dylan a few more shots of rum and Coke and an extra masseuse! Then I talked on into the evening...

Child Evictions

NONE OF THE neighbors really liked us and the reasons were many. But once in a blue moon we would try to play together. That was almost always a mistake. Bennie and I got into a war with two of the neighborhood kids. We were throwing dirt and rocks in an attempt to make the other team retreat inside their house in defeat. After our opponents had disappeared I went looking for them. I found one of the kids and hit him in the face with a wad of hard dirt. He ran home bleeding from the mouth. Being that his mom wanted no dealings with my crazy mom she got the landlord, Mr. West, involved. Mr. West would come down to address Mom about my actions. Mom was standing in the door talking to Mr. West while I was quivering behind the scenes. Mr. West told Mom that she could stay in the Red Line Community but I had to go. My heart was pumping times twenty. How was he going to throw me out? Where would I go? I was scared senseless! I knew my options of leaving and locating another place to live were slim to none! And of course, slim wasn't a friend of mine. That moment steered me straight going forward!

Remember My Name

SHOOTING MARBLES WAS more of a sport and a gambling addiction. A lot of parents didn't allow their kids to play the game due to the similarities.

So eventfully I joined "stick ball" like the other kids. I thought I did quite well but it was only a rubber ball with no glove. My best friend, Hill Harris, would talk me into playing organized baseball at the age of ten. He joined a national fast food chain (BKC) that sponsored one of the local teams. I thought it couldn't be much different from what I had been doing. Oh boy, was I ever so wrong! I totally sucked at it. I was the worst player on the team. I was probably close to being the worst player in the entire league. It was a league that consisted of about ten teams. Since the squad was short of players I got to participate, even though it was pure comedy to everyone except my teammates. The coach would place me in right field with the hope that no balls would come my way. However, when a ball did appear the coach's suspicions were correct. I would drop the ball or boot it badly.

When at bat, coach even ordered me to squat so as to decrease my strike zone. I couldn't hit a ball if you held it right in front of me! It was a complete disaster. What kept me around was my friendship with Hill Harris. Plus, I had nothing better to do at the time. We ended the season 2nd in the league with no thanks to me. It became more obvious that no one wanted me back the following year.

I took deep offense to being the laughingstock of the league. During the offseason I got Bennie to work me out as much as possible.

I just wouldn't quit! Every day I begged him to pitch to me and throw me balls again and again until he couldn't stand it anymore. I was going to matter in that league! I was going to get my redemption when the season started again.

We moved to another section on the Southside. I started working out with the area team, U.M. Baptist Church. It was quite a long walk to my old practice site. My old team wasn't providing many details either! They definitely didn't want me back.

U.M. Baptist Church couldn't believe their luck! I was a badly needed piece to their chance of competing. A deal was made with my old team and I became the newest member of U.M. Baptist Church team. I was happy but that was not enough. I couldn't wait to restore my image!

On opening day we would play the late game after my old team had performed. Seeing me at the park again gave them so many laughs and so much relief that I wasn't with them anymore. But rumors were already swirling that I wasn't the same player as I was the previous year. Almost no one was buying it though! As my teammates and me took the field, I slowly marched out to the shortstop position. The shortstop was like the quarterback of the infield. It would also place me dead center to all the major action. There I was "the operator," not the guy hidden away in right field. I could hear the snickers and questions by everyone who remembered my comedy show. The old teammates stayed around just for the jokes and amusement.

It didn't take long for me to assert myself. I was diving after would-be singles and making them outs! I was rushing bunts and gunning down runners! My batting was like a veteran to the game. Then I took the mound to close out our victory. Before the game was over my ex-coach was fighting with my new skipper. The old coach felt he had been suckered into trading me away. It was a moment that I have mentally framed into my forever memory! I walked away with a secret smile on my face. I had proven so many people wrong! I had overcome my fears as an eleven-year-old. That was an accomplishment that cemented my confidence and my self love.

Give Me That Old Time Religion

BASEBALL HAD MY interest but mom and Aunt Kathy had other plans for me. In the South kids had to commit their life to Christ between the ages of ten to twelve years old. After all, I thinkJesus had gotten baptized at the age of twelve. Bennie had gone through that process (REVIVAL) at the age of thirteen. Aunt Kathy was not going to allow me to go beyond the normal ages before I got baptized.

I had to stop playing baseball. I had been making quite a name for myself. The toughest part was that the church was only a block away from the ball park. I could hear the cheers and the commotion loudly from the church grounds. I was not a happy camper. Yet I had no choice in the matter.

The process would start with kids being secluded from television and secular music for two weeks. During that time they should pray and pray while asking Jesus to be saved. Evidence of being touched by the Holy Spirit had to be witnessed by One: a relative, while the candidate was at home in meditation. Two: A show of raw emotion during Revival service! Three: The Walk of Faith!

If a candidate was recommended by a relative (Option 1) then it had to be a well-respected member of the church. Option 2 was the Gold Standard. The congregation lived for a fiery confirmation of faith. It appeared to be the sole reason members attended night after night. Kids would be singing, dancing, crying, and screaming after being touched by the Holy Spirit! The Faithfuls would jump at the chance to be seen escorting an emotional candidate to the pastor's pulpit!

Option 3 was just a show of confidence. It was an implied statement that 'I'm a Christian and I know it!'

Next, the candidates would be baptized on the 2nd Sunday of Revival. The final step was the sharing of bread and wine, which was called Communion.

The Revival was a second chance for kids to redirect their lives. By repenting and accepting Jesus Christ, then all of our misdeeds and bad conduct would to be washed away.

Even I was hoping to be forgiven! My sordid reputation was certainly out there.

Once the service started, the congregation would sing while the candidates prayed. When Bennie went through the process he got up from prayer and started to dance and cry until Aunt Kathy escorted him to the pulpit, signaling he was ready for baptism. So I knew how that process should play out.

It took three days before I became full of emotion and the Holy Spirit! Suddenly I started to scream and dance! "YES Jesus, YES," I shouted! Again and again I screamed and I cried, "It's you, Lord, It's You"! I twisted and danced for what seemed to be five minutes to eternality! No one and I mean no one even dared to come to escort me to the pastor's pulpit. Neither Aunt Kathy nor Mom would come for me! As the service ended for the evening I was left standing all alone. Even my walk home was just me and a cold feeling of rejection. I couldn't even walk by the ball park because I felt so low. I kept asking myself, "Did I need to break dance or moon walk in order to get escorted! Why was I left out there to embarrass myself? As I got closer to home I remembered the three options; Witnessed by a relative, physical escort by a member, and the Walk of Faith! No one would have valued Mom's confirmation that I had received Jesus as my savior. That was not a good option. It was obvious that neither Aunt Kathy nor a church member could be relied upon as an escort. It was apparent that my only option was The Walk. That was it! I needed to Walk myself into the pulpit.

So I had it all planned out. I would wait until the kids were down in prayer. Then I would get up and "WALK" myself into the pulpit. That was just what I did! After the kids stood up from prayer, I was in the pulpit staring down at them. I wanted to show a smile but everyone especially the adults took those moments very seriously so I needed to shield my happiness. Next, I had to get through the Baptism. Then Communion was the final stage before my return to baseball.

I was baptized in the name of the "The FATHER,the Son, and the Holy Ghost" by Pastor Lloyd. I was excited because the end was near. Finally, I only needed to return that night for the eating of the bread and drinking of the wine.

As the evening drew near I wasn't feeling well due to something I had eaten. I felt terrible but I was determined to get that revival thing behind me.

There I was on the 2nd row being recognized as one of the newest servants of God. Pastor Lloyd would lead the church in Communion.

He said, "Take this bread as it is my body," Just as Jesus said in the Bible. I bit down on what appeared to be a small cracker. I was sick but I was able to stomach the cracker. Next, Pastor Lloyd said, "Drink this wine for it is my blood." As I attempted to swallow my shot glass of wine I vomited like a baby stuffed with sour milk. I really flooded the place. As Mom took me out of the church I could hear my naysayers saying, "I told you that boy didn't have the SPIRIT!" Nevertheless, I was somehow accepted as the latest member of Zion Union Missionary Baptist church. And most importantly I would be on the baseball field the next day.

Out of nowhere Dylan gave me a HIGH FIVE! We both smiled and tipped our alcoholic glasses while I attempted to entertain him even more.

The Coach Goes Rogue

AFTER LITTLE LEAGUE baseball I faded quickly in sports. I wasn't very big to begin with but all the athletes were getting much bigger, stronger, and faster than I. I was still the sandlot hero but that was nothing compared to my classmates from other districts. I had to let that dream go and find another way to exploit my love for sports.

I gave up working at the age of thirteen. I had done so many odd jobs since I was eight years old that I was simply burned out. I needed to do more at school rather than bouncing from classroom to work every day. I needed a cover to be away from Mom. Being the team trainer would be that sanctuary. I would get to be around sports. I would get to travel around Mississippi, which I had never done. I would make new friends that could help me get to school and back home for free. And finally, I would get the jump on Mom. By the time I returned home she would be quietly in bed.

No one knew I was an avid distance runner. I would jog almost daily around the football field at Mississippi University for Women just to clear my head. MUW was a female college (now a co-ed school) with a small sized football field. With training, I could have beaten all the long distance runners on our track team. My drawbacks were: One, my self esteem or fear of ridicule if I attempted to try out: And Two, I had a personal run-in with the track coach. He had strong-armed me for revenge after a joke was leveled at him by one his own runners. Instead of dealing with that person he took it out on me. I saw excelling as a way of helping him rather than competing just for myself. I still regret my failure to participate! Yet our confrontation became such a mental wall for me.

As I got closer to my high school graduation another sports coach approached me about receiving a scholarship to East Mississippi Junior College at Scoba, Mississippi as a team trainer. I simply told him thanks but no thanks. I had other plans at that point. The manager gig had served its purpose. It was time for me to grow up, move on, and evolve into the man I wanted to be.

The Chosen One

GROWING UP IN the church had so many dubious effects on me. I was ringside to the many dealings, the many cliques, and the many outtakes that unfolded right before me. There would be confessions after confessions where the same people would confess to something different a few weeks later. Honestly, my mom and Aunt Kathy should have made me a regular but their focus was elsewhere. There would be "testimony time" in which someone would affirm the grace of God had either helped them or saved them. Since I was a 'destruction in the flesh"; I should have been the opening or the closing witness during that time as well!

My Aunt Kathy never missed church or Bible study. She was like a government check. She was always going to be there. It never mattered where I sat, I could feel her steely eyes. Her voice was never on key. She would be pushing her own tune in the middle of the choir's performance.

As soon as we departed the parking lot Aunt Kathy would berate any and all members. There would be statements like "Deacon Skip is a son-of-a-dog," or "Sister Sally is a horse's ass," or "the building committee are a bunch of bastards..."

I always wanted to remind her that she was stepping on toes because another bastard was present.

I turned to Dylan and said, "My view of the pastor and his sermons were a complete opposite of the given intent." As he spoke, the women would be twitching and passing out. They would stand up and shout or they would stand up to dance. The pastor could change his volume and it stirred the congregation, especially the women!"

Because I had "no game" and got no attention, I would be sitting there trying to sponge off of him.

I said, "Dylan, he had it all: the looks, the voice, and the charisma!" Throw in a robe, a book, a piano, and a backup choir and even I could have made a splash when I knocked on a girl's door. Needless to say, none of this fell into my repertoire, even though I wished I could have used some of that fire and brimstone on a date.

The things I saw and the things I heard were reasons my relationship became casual with the church. I managed to escape without spilling my inner guts. At least that's what I thought!

After high school my friends and I would party all weekend and miss church on Sunday. Out of nowhere we developed this guilt complex about being absent from the services. We wrote down our respective places of worship and drew a church's name from a hat. It came up New Side Baptist Church. That would be our place of redemption. Unbeknownst to any of us, the selected church was never attended by the guy who dropped the winning name. Since I was the oldest, I was made the spokesman. We agreed on a day and time to make our appearance at New Side Baptist church.

We gathered out front of the church. We wanted to file in as a unit. And of course we wanted to sit together. I was the most savvy, so I would lead the way. We were nicely dressed with blazers, ties, and hard bottom shoes. The usher greeted us at the door then walked us to the very front where he sat us across from the minister. That should have been the first alert that something was unusual about our visit. Yet, we were eating our own hype. All eyes were on us like incoming rock stars. Secondly, I heard someone gleefully say, "There they are" as we passed through the aisles. Once again, I took it that the congregation was excited to see new faces. New guests always mean potential new members. As we took our seats there were sneers and looks of disgusts. Being confused and abashed, I couldn't wait for a hymn or a sermon, or just anything to get the attention off of us.

The preacher came to the podium and requested that we stand and introduce ourselves. He started with me. I told where I lived and where I had previously attended church. An old lady off to the side made a distressful shout: "That's Ms. Liza's boy!"

Suddenly, there was a grumbling and rustling coming from the pews. I looked toward the old lady and smiled in the affirmative. My friends gave their details. Everyone professed to be Christians. Afterward, I was asked to remain standing. Then it was just me going one on one with the pastor! It was obvious that he didn't know any of us. It became more obvious that we or shall I say, "me" was his sermon!

With me still standing, he accused us of being the dread of Columbus! I was shaking my head "No, no!" but the crowd was roaring "Go ahead now, go ahead" back to the preacher.

He then stated, "These sinners are stealing our future!" The crowd roared back again, "Take your time, pastor. Take your time!"

About that time I was looking to my friends for support! They had thinned out and left me alone as the "sacrificial lamb". The pastor took his finger and swiped left and right along our seating. As he locked onto me he swiped up and down, saying,"Here are the pushers, dope users, crack heads, meth heads, acid heads, pot heads, coke heads, and Lucy with Diamond heads!" This man was in a zone. There was no stopping him! Of course he meant LSD with his "Lucy with Diamond heads" reference but who was I to correct him? Yet the crowd responded with a loud gasp and a crescendo of,"Lord, help them! Lord, help them! Amen, pastor, amen!"

Inside I was protesting "NO NO, NO AMEN, NO AMEN, NO!" It was useless. So I gave up trying to fight him off. We were just his fish and his loaf of bread to feed to his flock. I had no choice but to take it. When the service came to a close we tried to mix into the congregation as we exited the building. I heard one last shot of repulse by the smallest attendant saying, "God be damn those backsliders!" As we reached our cars we scattered like roaches exposed to the light. Our efforts of repentance had turned into a crucifixion.

Dylan had fallen off his table while spilling Thai rum all over himself. I said, "Dylan, hey, hey! Be careful, you're spilling the good stuff!"

Dylan returned, "I should blame you and your stories for my clumsiness."

Social Healing
Hooky 101

I ALWAYS LIKED school. It was probably because I could control how much attention I got. Plus, there was nothing at home for me to do. I had no real friends, no toys, and no cable TV. There wasn't much food around the house either. So I looked forward to the free lunches. I would never miss a day during my four years of high school.

However, in the 2nd grade, Bennie talked me into shooting hooky. At the time we lived across from the Palmer Home orphanage. We made a hut out of straw with tree branches just inside of the Palmer Home ranch. Our plans were to hide there until Mom left for work. Everything was going as planned until we got a surprise visit. Some older dropouts were watching us when we entered our make-shift hut. They crashed our tepee and forced us out to face them!

I don't remember the names of all the guys but one of the them was called Emp-man. I had seen Emp-Man around the community many times before. He had a cone-shaped head like a watermelon. Without seeing the rest of his body I would have mistaken him for a leftover Jack-O-Lantern! He looked like a throw-away cartoon. He talked like he was choking on his words.

Emp-Man ordered his guys to tackle Bennie and me before we could escape. Next he was standing above us and dropping his pants! I nearly crapped my underwear, cried like a baby, and squealed like a pig! I had seen male packages before, of course. That didn't startle me. I was a naughty kid that knew of many demented hood-rats. Even my classmates would play a game of "Who could pee the furthest?" I had never won that contest but I was ok with my presentation. As a matter of fact I had accidentally seen some of my mom's boyfriends relieving themselves outside the house on several occasions. So seeing a man expose himself was nothing new. It was the idiotic assault that had my full attention!

There wasn't a doubt in my seven-year-old mind that they would have to kill me first! Yes, I was scared beyond words but I was not going out like that!

If Emp-Man had known my dilemma he would have continued on his way and wished we had never crossed paths! I was thinking of punching him in his package as hard as I could, then making a run for it! I'm sure they would have chased me down and beaten me beyond recognition. But I was audacious like that. The only thing that saved Emp-Man's balls and my ass was my concern for Bennie. Unlike myself, I wasn't sure that he was willing to take an ass beating.

So I relented for Plan B. I wasn't quite sure what that was at the time. But we definitely needed a God send or a sign from heaven. The group brought us to our feet and stared at us like we were hamburgers and French fries. They were either sizing us up or hoping that we gave in. Bennie and me were still in shock. We never said a word during the whole ordeal. Thankfully Bennie was holding strong because the thought of a hit and run just wouldn't leave my head!

They became somewhat concerned because of the morbid fear on our faces! I was hoping they would turn us loose, thinking they had impressed us! Bennie and me locked eyes, wishing we could shoot out like chickens without a head! But they would catch us within seconds. They were just too big and too fast for our elementary legs. Like a prayer out of nowhere Mom was heard leaving the house right on schedule! Just as the door slammed we started screaming, "Mom, Mom, Help! Mom, Mom Please Help!"

Emp-man and his boys vanished faster than they had appeared. I never saw any of those guys ever again. And that was the first, the last, and the only time I would shoot hooky away from school! Looking back I realized that Mom was a necessary evil that kept most of the predators away!

Dylan was lying on his back as the staff fanned him with over-sized palm leaves. I could tell he wasn't so certain about me and my childhood history. I purposely stared in Dylan's direction and said, "Don't worry mister, I'm not Catholic!" Then I proceeded on with my stories.

Dead Eye Red

I WAS AROUND eleven years old when my playmates and I started to openly talk about girls. Growing up in the hood allowed us to be closer to bad apples more than a kid should have been. Of course, we heard all the cuss words and all the demented propositions. I happened to notice that some people lived for those moments. There was no bigger showstopper than a lady called "Dead Eye Red." It's been more than forty-five years but my ears still burn with those thundering crescendoed chants of "Red, Red, Red" by the men at our local juke joint. They would be commanding this provocative Red Bone Vixen to get up and work the crowd.

I never knew her real name. But she was the talk of the tavern. She was a paying customer like everyone else but if Dead Eye Red was present, then the club literally belonged to her! She would always head to the center of the club to sing, dance, and flirt with the audience. She was more than a handful. She was what we would call Slim Sexy with a tight little butt. She wasn't much on the eyes. But her body and her seductive behavior kept all the wandering eyes peering her way. Even the women! She wore a red wig that made her look like an animal in heat. She had a lazy right eye. You couldn't tell if she was looking at you or ignoring you. Therefore, she got the nickname "DEAD EYE RED." She was much too old and way out of our league. Her desire to be out front even caught the gaze of all the young perverts. Mind you, we had no business being around Dead Eye Red or a tavern but she was way too much entertainment to stay away from. We would give any and every excuse to get near the bar just to see her show.

The tavern was off limits at night so we could only watch and listen from across the street. But during the day we could enter the tavern for potato chips, pops, pin balls, and billiards. If Dead Eye Red was in club then it was worth it.

She had to be about thirty-five years old at that time in my life. She was a chain smoker who drank far more than she should have. If her mouth was open, then she was swearing. She was definitely not the girl any man would take home to Mom. But music, liquor, and men revved her up like a steel locomotive.

We could hear her singing her own songs and out-talking everyone in sight. All the single men and even the married ones would line up just to dance with her. She would be spanking her own little butt as she worked the floor. There would be threats, fights, and shouting matches for a chance to dance with her. Dead Eye Red loved every minute of it. It was her house unless one of the guys had a date or a wife in the place. However, the presence of other females never slowed her down. And that was a problem! Women would beat her butt weekend after weekend. She would get bloody noses, busted lips, and scratches to the face. Or we would see her folded over from being punched in the gut. Trouble didn't follow Dead Eye Red. It walked step for step alongside her. Understandably, she would be banned for a small period of time. But the men would stay away in protest until Dead Eye Red was allowed to return. Once her restrictions were lifted then the bar came alive again.

Dead Eye Red would come back in the club to mock the owners with her singing, grinding, and dancing. Her go-to song was," I'm up in here. I'm just like a dog wagging my tail. I'm up in here"!

The men would egg her on with chants of "Red, Red, Red" as she danced and shook her small behind. If you wanted to catch her best, then you had to be there before she got drunk. She was the essence of Josephine Baker. Once her liquor set in, then her gyrations were like a broken machine. There wasn't much grooving to see, and nothing mesmerizing taking place. But she would be too drunk to know that.

It would be all silliness at that point!

On one occasion this guy went as far as to tell Dead Eye Red that he broke into her house that morning. She replied in a joking manner, "Oh really, what did you take?"

With all the ears sharply on him he told her, "I am now wearing your dirty underwear!"

She stopped, frowned, joined in the laughter, and then said, "I stole those panties too!"

After this exchange the club got louder and more people joined in the fun.

Dead Eye Red wasn't too good at holding her whiskey, but she lived to drink. And she drank just to drink. Before long they would be dragging her out of the bar minus her red wig. Yet, she had no shame. As soon as she was able to stand she was back at her old tricks.

As I got older I saw less and less of old Dead Eye Red. When I was nineteen years old my friend (J.B.) and me were returning from the mall when he spotted a familiar face walking home on a wet winter day. He signaled for me to turn around because he recognized the lady as Dead Eye Red. She was never the face of a sugar kiss beauty queen. Time had been cruel to her. All of the smoking, drinking, and socializing had taken a toll. She spoke more softly than I remembered. She even completed some sentences without a cuss word. Naturally I assumed that she had lost her wit along with her coke bottle figure. As she got in, I cordially mentioned that my back seats were very hard and very cold. Dead Eye Red responded, "Son, when I was young I could sit on a seat like this and smoke would appear!" I looked at J.B. and he looked at me. I knew it was time to get Dead Eye Red to her destination as fast as I could.

The Mourning Bench

OUR 6TH GRADE class was a trailer away from the main building. The disobedient kids would be put outside to sit and wait for corrective actions by our principal. We named this seat "The Mourning Bench"!

In the southern church the Mourning Bench was where you would pray and prepare for a signal from the Holy Spirit that recognized you as accepting Jesus Christ as your savior. None of us wanted to be whipped and especially by the principal. We would have accepted the Easter Bunny as our Prince of Peace if it would have saved our rear ends.

Our principal was nothing to play with. Rumor had it that he had been injured in war and that he was left shell shocked. Today "shell shock" would be the equivalence of Post Traumatic Stress Disorder (PTSD). Admittedly, we were too naive and too stupid to understand the seriousness of such a condition.

Our principal was the type of guy that would allow you to start your story or start your lie about why you were sent to his office. He would maintain a calm demeanor and sometimes even a smile as you laid out your lie! He would engage you and sometimes mislead you to hold to your story while he reached for his paddle or searched for his belt. Once you crawled deep within your lie he would snap and commence to beating you. It was completely useless to try to talk your way out of any ordeal. So we named him "shell shock." We were so afraid for our lives if we were discharged to see the principal. No one just hung out at his station. There were always kids crying before beatings and kids crying after beatings. Sounds of chaos, calamity, and despair echoed out of Shell Shock's post. Hell had to be a better option. If you were called out for misbehaving, then a path would open for your exit from the classroom. Kids would make low brow remarks, snickers, and hand gestures about your upcoming punishment. Fights would ensue on the way to see the principal. If you acted out on the way to see Shell Shock, then you got two scoops. One beating for your initial infraction and another beating for fighting.

Every fifty minutes or so the principal would make the rounds to discipline those unfortunate students. As luck would have it, I had finished my test sooner than my other classmates, yet I continued to talk and disrupt the class. I was sent outside with the PROBLEM kids. There were four people already awaiting their fate.

A classmate named Doug stayed in perpetual trouble for lying. He was a regular that managed to stay out of trouble on that day. Doug was a kid with tall tales and make-believe adventures. He was determined to impress us no matter what he had to do or what he had to say.

The four on the bench were two girls and two guys that were at least two or more years older than I was. Fearing that I would be beaten and bruised by Shell Shock, I had to put together a plan of action. My clothing was too thin and too cheap to protect the skinny bones I had! Unless the Easter Bunny made an immediate appearance, and soon, then nothing I could say was going to save my rear end.

I magically talked the other kids into hiding out for about twenty minutes until Shell Shock made his disciplinary rounds. For that moment I truly thought I was good at being persuasive! I was too green to realize that these four had other ideas long before I opened my big mouth.

So we sneaked off amongst the brushes and the trees. While in retreat the two guys and two girls started romancing each other. I was like Holy Cow, Wow, how did this happen? I created this scheme—now I'm made the Lookout!" For additional insult, the love scene went back and forth minus yours truly. And again and again I was at a loss as to how I drew the short straw! Regardless of the setup it was time to move on. So I gave word that Shell Shock had made his pass. We went back to our class with our best Oscar-winning faces. As we entered our classrooms, we knew how to look as if we had been whipped, battered, and beaten as we entered the room.

After school I told Doug about this wild adventure. I should have known better but the events of that day were way too much even for a young idiot like me! I made Doug swear not to tell anyone. One slip of the tongue and we would be facing Shell Shock. Then neither God, nor Satan, nor the Easter Bunny could have helped us!

I'm sure that story was far better than any lie that Doug could conjure up. He wasn't going to swallow such a story that didn't involve him. Like a kid at Christmas, Doug sprinted off to tell anyone and everyone that he thought would listen. Doug spoke in much graphic detail about him romancing the two girls! Words spread quickly. The parents of the two girls had the guys picked up and questioned with reference to assault.

The police stopped at Doug's house for the biggest and final piece of the puzzle. He tried to flee before being questioned. Even Doug's mom tried to corral him. The poor fool was dripping in tears while screaming, "Mom, it wasn't me, it wasn't me! They are lying on me."

Thinking that he was facing Reform school he suddenly gave a jailhouse confession! He would come clean and he was eventually released. The other boys were let go as well due to age and consent. Luckily, I was never accused nor taken in. Doug had told a lie that came back to bite him in the butt! And I I got my first initiation at being the 5th wheel!

Losing Gloria

I BECAME FRIENDS with Barry Ellison who had moved to Columbus from Chicago during the summer of the 5th grade. We were heading to the same grade even though he was about a year and a half older than I. He was a unique character. He had what seemed to me a unique mindset. He had more life experience than I had. I could out wrestle much bigger opponents but Barry taught me hand movements like a boxer. Then I really knew how to protect myself if needed.

We connected on a lot of levels. I would stay over at Barry's house for days on end. My mom would never question where I had been. However, I felt guilty for being away from my brothers. I was eating more, sleeping comfortably, and watching all the best television shows. I never told Barry why I would refuse to hangout but many times the guilt was just too overbearing! Barry's mother even bought me my first brand name shoes (Lew Alcindors). It was mind-blowing for me to finally have such quality shoes.

I started to learn about girls, fashion, and socials from Barry. It was a much different period of my life because I wasn't fighting every day. Barry never joked about my mom! He never sided against me. He was as solid as a real brother!

We also became friends with a classmate named Gloria. She would invite us over on the weekends for talks, music, and dates to the movies. Gloria was tall, cute, and sexy. If it wasn't for Barry I would have never gotten to know a charmer like Gloria. Of course, Barry had a thing for her but she kept him at arm's length. Gloria had many admirers. Mostly guys that were much older than either of us.

Gloria taught Barry and me about dating. She taught us how to dance. She gave us a swag that we badly needed. It was such incredible experience for me but probably just a normal thing for Barry. Nonetheless, she was a constant friend for about two years. Gloria would look out for us and we would look out for her. We became a tandem that no one understood.

Barry and me would leave for a weekend outing with his family to Quitman, Mississippi while abandoning Gloria for a couple of days. We promised her that we would catch up on lost time with her once we got back home.

Barry and I would have an amazing time on our getaway. Once we got to Quitman we stayed at his aunt's and uncle's home which used to be a funeral parlor. We were spooked silly from beginning to end. This home was very cold with few windows. There was a back room that had leftover coffins. There were makeup stands and jars of formaldehyde.

As if that wasn't enough, Barry's uncle would tell us that a ghost had lived in the home. There was a bullet hole in the door where Barry's aunt had tried to chase the ghost away.

Neither Barry nor I slept a wink the whole weekend. We stayed close to one another. We were in complete survivor mode! We spent most of our days playing outside until we were forced to come in. It was hard to eat! It was even more difficult to go to bed. There were constant sounds of creaky doors, slamming windows, dripping faucets, and power failures. We were so quiet and obedient. Barry's aunt and uncle also kept us in check with stories of the dead.

I had many experiences with cemeteries but this was much closer than I wanted to be. Barry and me tried to keep each other up from dusk to dawn. We would talk ourselves to sleep. If Barry fell asleep before me, then I would slyly nudge him just to keep him awake! On our second night we became alarmed because the carpet was moving. After mustering some courage to investigate, we saw a large house rat hiding under the bed! We broke down the bedroom door trying to escape! We were then punished with another ghost story for our senseless act!

The following day Barry dared me to get into one of the caskets. I was stupid, broke, and getting bolder by the day. I took Barry's money while creating a connection with the dead. Our getaway became a hoot from that point on!

Little did Barry's relative know that I was about to turn the table unlike anything they had expected.

I noticed the corner market had refrigerator magnets in the form of Voodoo dolls. I wanted a souvenir for my time in Southern Mississippi. Since I had won Barry's money I was able to afford the memorabilia that I wanted.

As I got back to Barry's aunt and uncle's home, I couldn't wait to show off my collection. When I pulled out the dolls everyone inside the house dashed out of sight! It was as if I had a skunk in my hand. I was forced to burn the dolls, gather the ashes, and bury the remains away from the house. They even made Barry and me ride in the front seat of the car on our return home just to keep an eye on us! Barry and me would slyly sneak a smile of approval from time to time. It was a smile of vindication. We knew that we had regained our manhood.

As strange as our weekend was, it suddenly turned tragic. Gloria had drowned while swimming with some older teenagers! The news was so shocking that neither Barry nor me ever talked about it. We never went to any part of her burial service. She was just gone!

I don't know why but I couldn't face Barry after losing Gloria! I felt guilty for not being there to protect her. I felt guilty for having so much fun when she needed us. I wasn't even sure if it was the Voodoo dolls. I was just hurt and I was numb.

Barry and I would eventually find new friends and grow apart. But Barry was by far the best boyhood friend I ever had!

The Wait!

AFTER THE NURSE pinched me, I was back to reality or shall I say "My Nightmare"? I was ready to go with the volunteer rescue team. I looked down at my thigh and I saw a cornrow of twenty stitches. I cautiously pulled my pants up as the onlookers smirked at me.

Hayward had summoned supporters to join in our employee search. Other contractors were busy ushering confused and disoriented workers back to the panic room. It was the most surreal thing that I have ever witnessed. We were still in imminent danger yet people were wandering about, seemingly unaware of what they were doing. Once again we had no trust in our Afghan security. We feared that turncoats were among them. Our distrust was so acute that some of the contractors took the guns away from the security guards.

It had been about two hours since the initial blast. Surely, the Marines or the QRF (Quick Reaction Forces) would have known about our predicament. Yet no one was in touch with us. We had no idea of what to do or where to go except to remain in our present area. If we were going to survive then it would be through our own will and our own determination.

Before joining the search party I ventured across the hall to get a coat. It was about 20 degrees Fahrenheit outside. The damage to my room was mild compared to others. Still it looked as if a tornado had visited the place. I had to feel my way around because the only light available was coming out of the panic room. I had lived there for six months but knew I was a complete stranger. I acquired more bumps and bruises by stumbling into every conceivable object strewn in the doorway. I got only far enough to grab a jacket before leaving what used to be my domain.

I hustled to catch up with the crew. The coldness of the night had set in. I could tell that my jacket wouldn't be enough but time was of the essence. So I pressed on while accepting that I would have to brave the elements. People's lives were in the balance so it would have been futile to turn back. By leaving the safety of the panic room I knew that I was putting myself in grave danger! Yet I knew Hayward and the crew would have done the same for me.

It didn't take long to realize that we were completely exposed to any and all hostilities. The Afghan guards I saw were not the ones I was accustomed too. The original security forces had dropped their guns and fled the facility like scalded dogs! Without question I was scared of any and all movements. I was scared of all stares. The thought of being gunned downed by potential posers weighed heavily on my mind at every turn. I was glancing fearfully at everyone. Especially those carrying guns. I was trying to find some type of facial recognition. I was trying to get an edge regarding where to run or where to hide should the situation turn tragic! That took me back to when I was nearly shot and killed in Mississippi.

Killer Crush

WHEN MY FRIEND Barry Ellison moved to the Northside I would visit him on occasion, which allowed me to connect with a lot of the kids in that section of town. Those friendships would serve me well, especially when the Southside thugs would fight the Northside thugs.

One of my neighborhood friends had a cousin named Ronny who would visit him on the Southside. He was four years younger than I and the rest of the guys. He was a quiet, handsome, but unassuming kid. At least that was what we thought.

During the summer of 1977 me and my friends would cruise the streets while listening to music, telling jokes, and admiring the girls. Our pack included Rob Jones, Jerry Pharr, and Edward Blount. When the darkness fell we would separate and try to visit our girlfriends.

On a quiet evening I dropped out of the crew and rode my bicycle over to the Northside to try my luck at romance. My girl and I decided to take a stroll around Hughes Elementary School. There were other kids out playing and hanging around the area. One of the most noticeable faces among them was Ronny. He was only thirteen years old whereas I was seventeen at the time. Unbeknownst to us he had a "KILLER CRUSH" on my girlfriend! Ronny had been spying on us as we toured the school grounds. When I became aware that he had been following us, I stopped and called him out. Ronny was holding a hammer-sized stick as he marched toward me. He was smaller so I figured I could subdue him if I had to!

Suddenly, Ronny stopped his progression while his boyz came between us! They tried to soothe the situation before we got into a fist fight. But Ronny disappeared before they could calm him down.

These friends of Ronny knew me as well, so they were making an honest effort to broker peace between us. I walked my girlfriend home while wondering what had gotten into Ronny. I had known of him for some time. I knew his older cousins for years. Also, he didn't stand a chance in a brawl with me. After I got my friend home, I was summoned back out to shake hands with Ronny as a gesture of "We're all good." However, Ronny looked me in the eyes, pulled out a knife, and said, "I'm going to get you when you leave!"

I kept my distance and without a missing a beat I said, "Ok, I will see you when I leave." As I walked back to my girl's house, my mind was racing. I was afraid but pretending to be unfazed. No doubt the situation had gotten out of hand without my really knowing all the particulars of Ronny's anger! I wanted to diffuse the situation but Ronny wasn't having it. So I had to devise a plan to get out of harm's way.

Even though I wasn't from the area I knew a couple of different routes to get back home. So I decided to wait until Ronny was relaxed, then I'd jump on my bicycle and make a dash for it. I'd worry about revenge at a later date. Of course, if he came to visit his relatives on the Southside then I would give him a real two piece (a left and a right hook butt beating)! First chance I got I hit the road, paddling like my life depended on it! Ronny didn't give up easily. He chased me for what seem to be four long laborious miles.

The next day I told Rob, Edward, and Jerry about my night of horror. They never said anything. They just allowed me to vent and fume over my desire to get Ronny back.

Time passed and Ronny never showed up at his cousin's house on the Southside. Me and the guys were out cruising one evening when we drove right past Ronny on the streets. He was walking at a brisk pace with a distraught look that I had only ever seen on my Mom's face! That was my chance to exact revenge on Ronny. He needed to feel some hard knocks for challenging me.

I told Rob, "Hey, stop the car! There's Ronny. So let me out."

Rob said, "No, we are not letting you out."

I appealed to Jerry and Edward to make Rob stop the car. They both said, "No man, let it go!" I was furious! What type of friends were these guys? I always had their back even when it was stupid to do so. As we got home and turned on the news we found out that Ronny had been arrested for shooting a guy in the area where we last saw him. Ronny had another "Killer Crush" on a different girl! Once again that girl was four years older than Ronny.

When we saw Ronny on the street he was still "at large" with his gun tucked neatly away in his pants. If Rob had allowed me to get out of the car, Ronny would have ended me on that day!

What's Yours Is Mine

AS I ENTERED college J.B. became my co-worker and my running buddy. I was four years older so I treated him mostly like a little brother but he was just good company and a good friend. He kept me laughing with his outrageous outtakes on life and relationships. I'd like to say that I was a good barrier between him and his hardships, but I wouldn't swear to that.

He would let me have it as well. Whenever I made miscues in my dealing with females, he would definitely pounce at the chance to embarrass me. He was always trying to outdo me at all costs!

One Christmas season I had bought my girlfriend a gift long before J.B. completed his shopping. So J.B. took it upon himself to try and top what I had bought. I was having too much fun watching him enter store after store trying to find something with which to outdo me yet within his price range. He finally settled on a very nice sweater that he had monogrammed with his girlfriend's initials. It was awesome but definitely a garment only for a lady. Admittedly, I was outdone but not jealous. I was happy for my friend. We delivered our gifts about two days before Christmas with contentment and joy. We just knew that we were the perfect elves for our sweethearts.

Of course J.B. wouldn't let it rest that he was the better Santa. I had to swallow being the runner-up. We decided to go out partying at a nearby club the night before Christmas. J.B. was all smiles and giving me grief about him topping my present. After being in the club for about an hour I recognized J.B. girlfriend's brother was also in the place with us. He was wearing the same monogrammed sweater that J.B. had bought his girlfriend! Apparently, the brother had either taken his sister's sweater or she had given it to him. Most definitely I was baffled as to why he would be wearing a female garment, especially with someone else's initials. However, I just had to see the look on J.B.'s face! I just had to see J.B.'s reaction to this guy wearing his girlfriend's sweater. J.B.'s response was beyond words! He was so shocked that he said nothing for the rest of the evening. He said nothing for days. I felt sorry for my friend. It was definitely 'a "God bless his heart" moment but I couldn't stop laughing. It took weeks before I could stop bringing it up. J.B. never teased me again. He knew I had the magic bullet to fend him off.

Flirty Shirley!

GROWING UP ACROSS from Friendship Confederate Cemetery allowed me to build a boldness in regard to graveyards. Friendship was like a park to us. We played hide-n-seek. We had bicycle races. We picked the plums that flourished near the river. This was a beautiful and solemn resting place. We meant no disrespect! We were just young and naive with nothing to do. I saw so many processions that I dreamt of getting that kind of send off. I'm sure my time spent in Friendship added to my darker side.

I told Dylan, "A graveyard saved me from Flirty Shirley!"

Dylan asked,"Who was Flirty Shirley?"

"She was only the most voluptuous creature to ever walk the earth. Nothing ever prepares you for a girl like Flirty Shirley. Neither Mom nor Dad would allow you to marry a girl like Flirty Shirley. Her bathwater was the appetizer and the chaser. She was as black as she was fine and as fine as she was black! She was not a teacher, or a homemaker, or an accountant. One look and you were never the same. Flirty Shirley appeared hotter each time you saw her. She was a pinup cast in an adolescent world. I got to know her during high school. I was a student and she was a diva! She had no academic drive or nothing of interest. But her presence was water in a desert. Her movements were a memory. She walked through your mind and stepped on your heart. She was a tormenter and she knew it! She was allure dipped in acid.

I was never her type! Flirty Shirley only dated athletes, actors, and men with money. However, we became friends. At least I was allowed to say that. I was delighted just to be around.

She used me and used me some more. I was her tissue when she had a cold. My car became her taxi with a smile. In college I made my play out of The Friend Zone. Flirty Shirley told me that she only dated "The Prime Cut"! It was crushing but we continued on. I would drop her off at clubs without question. Once inside the music would stop and she would be introduced. Flirty Shirley was the champagne! Her twisting and twirling were illegal by most standards.

In between shuttles I created dates. I had to take my shot at this goddess. I worked on my footwork and my flow. I was ready for Soul Train. I took her dancing. She would leave without me!

I took her to dinner. She ordered three full entrees! I was smashed! I delayed our departure. I had to see her gulp it down.

Flirty Shirley was in my system like a rare disease. She would surely be my damnation if I continued. There had to be a sign. There had to be a cure for my addiction!

After dinner I kicked myself. I was below my dignity. I was just gum on her shoes. I was a better man but what was I doing!

As I drove I thought and I thought as I drove. I passed through one light after another. I needed an intervention. I needed to reject her spell over me!

I was in anguish. But she was singing and rapping. I had to stop for gas. I could see a churchyard in the distance. A place to clear my head I thought. As I entered the gates, Flirty Shirley swiveled to the left and to the right. She asked, "What are you doing and why are we here?" I told her I needed a moment. "A moment…a moment for what?" she said.

As I got out, Flirty Shirley quickly hit the locks! I walked about while she was banging on the doors. She was flashing the lights and tooting the horn. I heard her noises but that was all. I shuffled about between the tombs. I read the stones. Flirty Shirley was frantically smacking windows and making promises.

It was time to go! My weight was lifted. I reached for the door and so did she. She wasn't letting me in. I attempted to leave and she uncorked a scream that rattled the dead.

I laughed until I almost cried! Her fear was too concerning. She relented and allowed me back into the car. As I drove off, Flirty Shirley was clenching my arm like never before. She was exhausted.

She would never speak to me again but I really didn't care. Her spell had been broken by the dead.

Ossie May!

DYLAN LOOKED AT me and said, "Dude, you are funny!"

I said, "You really think so!"

He then asked if I had anymore weird dates.

"As a matter of fact I do," I replied.

Dylan laughed at me some more. Then he said, "Let's hear them." I was so glad that he went there.

I met Ossie May on the way to work. In reality she met me by forcing me off the road. She cornered me and asked my name and number. That should have been a clue but I was lonely and new to Memphis. The first date was like talking her off a ledge! She went full meltdown. I took her home, vowing never to see this woman again. My pledge had just one major flaw. She knew where I lived. She showed up the next day. And the next! And the day after that! She knew my friends and my co-workers. There was no getting rid of her!

There was nothing ordinary about Ossie May. She was tall, sexy, smart, and pretty. I wish could stop right there, but her looks and personality were her drawing card.

The flip side was her temperament. She must have invented cussing. She would unload swear word after swear word in rapid succession. There had to be a law against such offensive language. She was always armed. She talked about her gun more than she bragged about her cooking.

Ossie May was just pure bad news! She was beauty and rage sandwiched together. She would show up unannounced. She would show up uninvited! She would show up just to show off. In other words, she was everywhere and nowhere I wanted her to be!

I had no choice but to see her. She was my bully and my stalker. She took me to the gun range. She finished one clip with her right then unloaded the other clip with her left. I certainly got the message. She was not to be messed with or messed over! I was scared straight by a woman.

Ossie May would make my schedule. She picked my friends. She enforced her curfew. She was preparing me for the O-M tattoo when suddenly I was rear-ended by an uninsured motorist. I was battling whiplash for six months. During that time I rediscovered myself. I had to give Ossie May the slip. Yet, no one had ever left Ossie May and survived. At least no one on record. I would be foolish to be the first.

Anyway, I waited for the right time. It would come at 3:00 a.m. in the morning. She called from work demanding that I take her home. I said, "Sure, I'm on my way." I knew it would be dicey but it had to be done. Normally, I would have rushed her home but I wanted to savor every minute.

Ossie May started her insults and threats as I drove down Horn Lake Road. She compared me to animals and idiots! She said words that I dare not repeat. Terms that Britannica, Webster, and Wikipedia wouldn't even allow! She was mid-sentence when she realized I had driven past a tombstone. She did a 360 then clutched my hand as the car rested between the crypts. She was as stiff as a board. I was in my element now. I was determined to change our course. I suggested that we get out. She replied, "Like Hell!"

I reached for her door and she grabbed at my hand. I told her to wait as I walked about.

Ossie May shouted, "That's bullshit!"

I felt more and more empowered so I decided to have more fun. I told her that I wanted to step out and gather her some flowers. She loudly stated, "I don't need or want any damn flowers!"

Out of fear she machine gunned a battery of swear words that I'm sure violate every cursing manual. Her profane assault came so fast and so intensely that I was literally ducking and dodging as she spewed out her garbage. She even used the same cuss word twice. Up until that point she had not attempted to harm me, yet I felt completely bruised and battered. I definitely needed relief.

Returning to the car, when I reached for my door, she collared my throat, pulled her gun, and took the keys. I grabbed her weapon and dared her to breathe! Ossie May turned to tears and whimpers that only a dog could hear. She begged and begged me to leave New Park Cemetery. I held strong until she promised to disappear from my life. Unsure of her seriousness I made her agree to take a day tour of the graveyard. Ossie May made an emotional vow to be there. She gave me a flushed look with her big watery eyes and said, "I will call you!"

It's been thirty-five years and I am still waiting by the phone.

The Big Cop-Out

I DIDN'T REALLY date until college. I just didn't have the stature, the personality, or the reputation that attracted females. My skill to interact with girls came mostly through television. Life versus Hollywood does not go hand and hand. I learned later in life that I had no game, no romance, and no joy about me in my younger years. I had what I called a "smell of desperation." Women could see it, detect it, and smartly ran away from it!

I had no viable role models especially in men. I hardly knew of any married people. My knowledge of relationships was comprised of gutter advice from the streets.

But I did meet Amber during the summer of 1982, after graduating from Mississippi State University. I dated her for more than a year. She was the love connection that I had longed for! But in time I find out that she was my apple and I was her lemon!

Amber was from a middle class family. I was the peasant from across the tracks.

In other words her parents initially didn't care for the young lover boy.

I modeled my appearance from images in JQ magazines. I thought I had a look above being a "Project kid" or a "Local bum." I even walked with an air of confidence.

The first time I went to Amber's suburban home I was dressed to the nines! But to her mother my attire was just lipstick on a pig. She wasn't buying the refurbished me. I actually felt like she had seen mud on my forehead. That woman cared less than two cents to even talk to me. I held my composure in spite of her snide remarks. I was uncomfortable but respectful. Her mother's put-downs were just water off of a duck's back.

I had gotten to know my dad in 1981. My dad was a well respected businessman in Columbus. A lot of families looked up to him. Even still, I never told anyone who my dad was. I wasn't sure how long our relationship would last. I didn't care for the drama of the non-believers nor any open conversations about him.

Out of nowhere Amber mentioned that I was seen in the Holly Hills section of the city. She wanted answers as to why I would be on her side of town. I finally gave in and told her I was out visiting my dad. The look on Amber's face was to die for! She would carry that new information back home to her parents.

The next time I went to Amber's place I was greeted at the door by her mother. This time I was welcomed and escorted to the Big Boy chair. I was offered drinks and hors d'oeuvres. Since it was Amber's birthday her dad insisted that I take Amber out in his Mercedes and not my hoop-d. I was shocked stupid! I kept my cool demeanor but underneath I was saying, "Holy, holy Jesus what is going on?" I had gone from the outhouse to the penthouse with a mere slip of the tongue.

I took Amber to a fast food joint and respectfully returned her home. We were out and back before her sisters even started their dates. Yes, I saw the disappointment on my girl's face but I had no money. I could only promise better things in the future. I did add, "Sweetheart, you do have the best man of them all!"

Amber and I would continue our long distance relationship well into the summer of 1983. I went on to attend Jackson State University whereas she remained at a local college. She had gotten into my system like no woman before. I was happy and determined to make her "THE ONE"! Little did I know our last date would be spent going out to dinner, to a movie, and a tour of Jackson, Mississippi. We were stupidly in love. At least that's what I felt. About a week later a friend would tell me that Amber was engaged to be married! It was poker face time but I was burning inside.

I told this friend, "Oh yes, I knew about her engagement. Amber was nothing to me!" I probably fooled no one but I didn't know what else to say. As soon as my friend was out of sight I was in overdrive, digging through my pockets for money to make a phone call! Just as I found the right amount I said to myself "Stop, wait a couple of days, then go to see her. Just make it a big pow wow! Something of this magnitude requires a face to face conversation."

A funny thing happened on my drive from Jackson to Columbus. I started to measure myself against this "unknown guy" That person had to have known Amber and her family for some time. So the betrayal factor was definitely in effect. That guy was in the military, which meant he had a steady job, whereas I did not. A soldier has a future that's constantly expanding, whereas my future was yet unknown. Plus, the old trump card of me being from across the tracks with the Crazy Mom that Rode a Bike" was a sure handicap!

If I was going to make a last minute play for Amber then I would need more than "Baby, I LOVE YOU"! By the time I got to Columbus I talked myself into retaining the little dignity I had left! So I decided to just make a call to congratulate my now ex-girlfriend, then be on my way, As soon as I got home I fought back my emotions and I did what had to be done!

Suddenly I heard, "That witch!" coming from Dylan! I looked up and Dylan said it again. "What a witch!"

I said, "No dude, I should have manned the hell up! I was NOBODY with NOTHING to lose so I should have fought for her"! Then Dylan said, "Sorry, I hit a soft spot, huh"?

I glanced back and answered "Maybe"! Then I said,"Hold on! There's more."

About ten years would pass and I was still puzzled how my Amber could have left me the way she did. I was certain Amber and I were breathing the same air. I would have sworn that our hearts beat in a rhythm. I would have bet that our taste buds were identical. It was a heartbreak that made me look unequivocally at me!

I had a thing for '70s R-n-B vinyl records. I was home on a Christmas Eve when I decided to visit the music store. There I was thumbing through the oldies when suddenly I noticed Amber standing face to face with me! Amazingly, she remembered my pastime. We hugged, we cried, and talked about our lives.

After breaking the ice it was obvious that our time had passed. But I had to know what really happened? I pleaded for an answer! Amber told me that she was deeply in love with me but she was also being molested by a family member! She said that she was tolerating his illicit behavior until he made a pass at her roommate. Something about those advances tripped her need to get far away! So when an old flame proposed marriage she quickly accepted. She said that proposition was an escape that she just couldn't afford to pass up. I wanted to probe her even further. Then I realized how painful it must have been to share that much of her soul.

I had found my Amber! I had gotten my closure! I kissed her on the cheeks. I got in my Mercedes. And I disappeared forever into the Mississippi Delta.

Dylan was just silent. He held his tongue for a while. Then he asked, "Are you ok"?

I cleared my eyes and said, "Dylan, let's move on."

"Sure", he said.

Tapping Out!

I GOT TO Memphis in the fall of 1987. I left behind the dream life of college where there were co-eds all around. Being a young professional in a blue collar city wasn't a good mix for me! I was miserable and I was lonely. Even the people I dated made me feel empty and depressed. It just wasn't a good place or a decent time for me when it came to social interactions. I was a loser and I knew it. It was probably the first time I accepted that I didn't have a knack for dating!

I met Adela through a co-worker. To this day I question the intent of that co-worker! Adela wasn't the sharpest knife in the drawer. To be honest I wasn't sure that she was all there. But she was sexy and a step up from some of the girls I had previously dated so why not give it a shot? She was also a religious zealot. Her friends and family were of the same mindset. They would always try to out-Christian" one another! If one person said, "Praise the Lord" then the other had to top it with "Praise the Lord and thank you, Jesus"! Or then someone may say, "HELP me LORD," then you would hear another voice saying, "HELP me LORD, You ANGEL of MERCY"!

It felt like a constant battle. If you were not from their "Faith" then you were never "good enough" or "Christian enough" for their acceptance. It just didn't matter who you were or what you did. If you didn't espouse their beliefs then you were on the Highway to Hell.

I wasn't stupid enough to introduce Adela to my relatives or my friends. She was the constant crusader. Given the chance she would have been spreading her gospel non-stop to each and every ear about the sins of mankind!

I had enough issues with my own family. They didn't need to know that I was slipping and sliding into the loony bin.

Trying to reason with Adela was like risking my own IQ. Each conversation made me dumber than the talk before. But I was a curious idiot! This was something totally different. There was just no explanation for my pursuit except being a man and a glutton for foolishness. It had been awhile since I experienced pure madness so my tank must have been running low!

I accepted the challenge to see where Adela would take me. Of all people, I should have known better. It was a casino-like experience. Even when you win you actually lose because gambling was now in your system!

Attending church was Adela's form of dating. I accepted her invitation because I wanted to impress her, plus I wanted to see it all for myself.

I was dressed and ready to go hours before the opening of service. I was not going to miss church that day. People were dancing, stumping, and shouting up and down the aisles! Adela was restless because she wanted to join in yet she was worried about my perception of her.

There was this member that they named "Sister Baba" that would roar like a truck engine whenever she felt the Spirit. Everyone would zero in and watch while anticipating her "Roar"! As expected, Sister Baba didn't disappoint. She sounded like a convoy! She really had the "hammer down." She could drown out the other parishioners all by herself. Everyone screamed and cheered in approval as if to say, "10-4 Little Sister."

I didn't say much after we left church. I knew the service meant a lot to Adela so I kept my opinions to myself. Without my approval Adela volunteered me as the church tamborine player. I had no interest in the job. I was even more dismayed that Adela threw my name in the hat.

Things would get tricky after that!

For Thanksgiving Adela persuaded me to drop her off at her parents' home in Indianola, Mississippi. I should have known that something was awfully strange when I picked her up. She had a distant and a silent aura about her. Yet still, I greeted her with "Hello pretty lady." But she only gave me a hand gesture in greeting. I tried several different openings but she said very little if anything at all. I didn't know if she was trying to ration her words or she had met her quota for the day. As I drove I talked about the beautiful countryside and the famous places along Highway 64 but I was only engaging myself. When I finally reached her parents' driveway she bolted out of the car to greet and to hug all of her relatives. I was left alone to drag all of her luggage to the door. What I didn't see was her severely mentally challenged brother approaching me like a pit bull! As I opened the trunk and started gathering the pieces I was suddenly attacked from behind. It was Adela's brother being protective yet putting me in a sleeper hold He was as strong as an ox! I was twisting and foaming at the mouth, trying to break his police grip. I had been in many fights before and I knew how to break a choke hold but to undo it would have required me putting a serious hurt on that guy! I decided to take one for the team. I knew if I put him down then my first impression would have been a hostile one. So I hung on until Adela's family subdued him! Either way, it was fair to say that I tapped out!

Run, Fight, or Stay?

MY CO-WORKER, JANICE Langford, invited me out for drinks in the fall of 1988. I had just bought a brand new sports car so I was excited to show it off. As a matter of fact, I was considering myself to be HOT COOL ICE! I drove with the confidence of a proud rooster. I wasn't dating anyone at the time so hope and temptation were smeared all over my face. It didn't take long before one of Janice's girlfriends was desiring to meet me. This girl was named Beverly. She had mocha skin with short hair and with big brown eyes. She had a rump that filled her pants like a Thanksgiving's day turkey. I felt luck had fallen upon me. We would exchange phone numbers before leaving the bar. After two phone calls she persuaded me to stop over for a sit-down conversation.

I got to Beverly's home around 7:00 p.m. on a Monday evening. Her residence happened to be in an older working class section of Memphis. I saw and heard no sound of kids in the area. She greeted me at the door with a smile that convinced me that I made a smart choice to pursue this Hot Cocoa of a woman. The house was notice-ably silent. Beverly never said that we were alone and I wasn't smart enough to ask.

I sat on the couch waiting for Beverly to get settled and break the ice. As I was getting acquainted with my surrounding there was a knock at the door. I gave a smirk then asked sarcastically if I needed to leave.

Beverly responded with, "No, you do not have to do that!" That wasn't the reply I was expecting. Nonetheless, my inner radar was pinging with "What does that mean and what have I gotten myself into?"

Beverly opened the door and in marched a young guy that appeared to be about my age with a similar physique. He addressed me with a smile and said, "You don't have to get up!" Now my heart and mind were racing. "What was really going on here?" I became instantly nervous!

This man took Beverly into the back room where I suddenly heard slaps, smacks, and grimacing sounds of abuse! As if that wasn't earth shattering enough, I heard the voice of an older lady. It had to be Beverly's mom pleading with this guy to stop hitting her daughter!

I was engulfed with fear and duplicity! I had no doubt that I could have taken this man. But I only knew Beverly for all of two conversations at best. I had no idea who actually owned the home! I didn't know the layout of the house. This guy had come in and out of the living room so fast that I couldn't tell if he had a weapon!

Obviously, this had happened before. The moms I knew of would have attacked or killed any man that assaulted their daughter. No doubt there was some type of relationship I had walked in on!

So there I was planted in the center of the floor trying to decide whether to fight or run. My legs were as heavy as two buckets of lead. I must have been sweating like a pig while anguishing over what to do!

"Get the hell out of there" was my decision. I just needed my legs to understand that. I had heard of freezing up before, but now I was living it! I couldn't move an inch. I was completely frozen in shock. Even the fear that this guy could return to attack me while I was nailed to the floor was overwhelming me.

Somehow and someway my blood reentered my lower half so I jetted out the door. I dashed to my sports car while trying not to fumble the keys. As I pulled out of the driveway the guy came rushing toward me with a devious smile of contentment. He was waving for me to stop. Like a two-time fool I obeyed. He walked closer to my car then said, "You didn't have to leave! That was only business." I looked him in the eyes and said, "Ok." Then I sped off like a bat out of hell. Enough was enough!

The next day I got a call from Beverly. I was waiting for her to scold me for not helping. I was listening for the details of her police report. I figured that someone would want to know how much I had witnessed. Beverly made no mention of that ordeal at all. She wanted to make another date. That's when I told her to "forget that she had met me and please lose my number!"

Stool Sample from the Stool Pigeon

EVEN THOUGH I wasn't much with the girls it never stopped me from trying. Before I got married I was encountering some intestinal problems. So I went to a Gastroenterologist for an evaluation. He ran a bunch of tests then asked me to see an Allergist. After we found no resolution I went back to the stomach doctor for another assessment. The Gastroenterologist asked me to drop off a stool sample at the desk of the emergency room. I was flabbergasted that he requested such a survey of my diet. The whole time I was wondering how in hell would I gather this specimen? How will I carry it? And what would I tell the emergency room representative?

Little did I know that my humiliation was only beginning. I won't say how I gathered my sample but I put it in a zip-lock container followed by a brown paper bag. I headed to the hospital for the drop-off just hours before my scheduled duty. As I walked into the emergency room I saw this beautiful sexy lady working the desk. I decided right then that there was no way in God's name that I was going to give this cutie my bag of crap. Secondly, I was smitten! I needed an opening to ask for her phone number. I knew if I had a smidgen of a chance, then I couldn't proposition her with a lunch bag of crap in my hand! I had to devise a plan. I decided to wait her out. I would sit until she went on break. If I guessed right, her replacement would be a little old lady. I would then make my drop and approach the pretty girl after her relief had moved my sample out of sight. To say I had rotten luck would be an accurate statement. Not only did this girl not take a break, I was running late for work. I was pacing back and forth like a stressed father waiting on the birth of his child. I was completely out of options. I had lost the battle of wills. With pain and trepidation I walked to the counter and presented this doll with my stool sample. I sheepishly kept my head down and headed out the door. I kept thinking about how that moment would have been a lasting stamp of her image of me even if I had succeeded! I was just imagining that she would've told me at some point that, "You were a bag of crap when I met you and you are still a bag of crap!"

Doing Hard Time

I SPENT A life of being conflicted about my dad. I started out majoring in education only to realize that education wasn't for me. I immediately changed directions. I was determined to have a career that paid better than the job of my dad.

In 1996 I had a defining moment when I was forced to accept the fact that I was exactly like my dad! I had his looks. I had his mannerisms. I had his humor. He was a very intelligent man. Ok, he had me beat there! But then I had a kid out of wedlock just like my dad. That realization shook me to the core. If I was a better father then I should try to be there for my kid.

Suddenly, the ball was in motion. I was determined to win back my baby's mama. I would make her my wife. It didn't matter if I loved her or not. I was going to shape my kid and protect my kid no matter what. I knew I was a damaged being! But it wasn't about me. My focus was on my kid and not my bride. It was an insane notion but I really didn't care.

Of course, it was just a matter of time for trouble to rear its ugly head. So in 1998 I got into a spat with my wife about the abuse of money. My wife had a concept that if she left the area when someone was upset then the argument would have to go away. If there was no one around to fuss with, then you would eventfully calm your own self down!

There I was demanding an explanation about her spending habits. Yet she was trying to avoid me. Unbeknownst to me, she had instructed our daughter to dial 9-1-1 if I touched her. After following my wife around the house I decided to grab her arm to make her face me. She jerked away and continued to walk to another part of the house. I gave up and decided to watch college basketball "sweet sixteens"! It was a Friday evening so I decided to relax in the comfort of the bedroom. I even unwound down to my T-shirt and boxers.

Within no time there was a ring at the door. It was the Memphis Police Department! They came in and asked questions with regard to domestic violence. That was only a few years after O.J. Simpson put the stamp on spousal battery. If the cops were called out, then they had to remove someone from the home. The Memphis P.D. saw a smear where I had held my wife's arm. Just like that, I was handcuffed while in my T-shirt and boxers. I desperately pled with the officers for more clothing. They finally relented and allowed me to grab a shirt and a pair of trousers. I don't think I was ready for the looks and temptations of wearing next to nothing! That would have been a busy weekend for me. God either saved me or some other fool(s) from having a near death experience(s) at the city jail!

For a man that had been humiliated by his mom for so many years, I was embarrassed; but that was minor compared to her Richter scale.

I was taken downtown and booked on charges of simple assault. It had been thirty-four years since my initial jail field trip behind bars. There would be no Mom to hold my hand! This time I had more company! I was placed in a cell of twenty-two people with one open toilet. I had to put my poker face on in lightning speed.

I was amongst real criminals or maybe small time offenders. I wasn't sure because I wasn't talking to anyone. For breakfast, lunch, and dinner we were served tuna and peanut butter sandwiches. I wanted nothing to do with that place. I wanted no food nor any conversations. Out of sheer luck or God's grace I didn't have to use the restroom for two days! But guess what? I wasn't going anywhere soon.

One of my cellmates noticed that I was turning down my food so he requested that I take the sandwiches and give them to him. I looked him in the face while thinking, "If I do that then what prison statement was I making?" I didn't promise him anything. I just covered my mouth and shrugged my shoulders in a maybe."

The guards were pacing to and fro while the cellmates were yelling to make phone calls or complaining of injuries. Sometimes it was just yelling for attention. I was doing my best to not make any eye contact with anyone. Out of nowhere the guards brought a new guy in with shackles on his hands and feet. This guy had on a paper jumpsuit! As much as I was trying to mind my own business I couldn't help but watch this guy. How or why did this guy have on a "Paper Jumpsuit"? I must have spent all of Friday evening trying to solve the mystery of our newest road dog! Years later I talked with someone in law enforcement about my cellmate's attire. I was told that he had to have been picked up for indecent exposure. The jumpsuit was his temporary wardrobe.

Saturday morning arrived and I hadn't slept a wink. I had given my cellmate my tuna sandwich but I was prepared to go to war if I had to! Amazingly it took only a few hours for me to be institutionalized! I was not going to be assaulted without retaliating with evil consequences.

Even though it was March, the number of people in the cell was unhealthy for all involved. So the guards let us out into the hallway to stretch for about two hours. During that time we tried to phone out to relatives or friends just to reach outside contacts.

I happened to be next in line to use the phone when this big female guard said for us to get completely away from it! She had to have known that we were using the service so why stop us now? More importantly, I was slated to be the next user. I tried to plead my case. The big guard stated, "If anyone says another damn word they will be back in their cell" I was just too close give up. I needed to see if my "one phone call" had gotten any traction! So I blurted out to the big guard "Ma'am, Ms. Ma'am, Can I just make one call?" The big guard screamed at me "Get your Damn Ass in that Damn cell!" She opened the bars and I walked in alone. I was like, "Wow, this is crazy" then I realized I was in the cell all by myself! It was like "Oh yes, I can get some sleep now!"

Later that Saturday night I was taken upstairs and placed in a cell all alone. As time ticked by I buried my head in my pillow and kept asking, "How in God's name did this happen?"

Finally, I was released on Sunday morning. My wife was there to pick me up. I said very few words. But I couldn't wait to shower, shave, and eat for the first time since Friday.

At my hearing my lawyer got my case expunged with the agreement that I would go to Anger Management. I thanked my attorney with a smile while thinking, "Love you, Jesus and No Problem, sir!"

Mad, Mad Money

I GOT TO my Anger Management sessions as early as possible. You would have thought I was applying for a new job. I was just determined to get that saga behind me!

There were twenty-two participants in the class. I looked around to see if any of them were ex-cellmates. We could have had a reunion. Yet, none of my "weekend dogs" were there. I guess they needed more "seasoning" at the ranch.

The instructor asked us to stand up, introduce ourselves, and state our infractions. Initially, I was bubbling inside. I felt I had been mistakenly taken in and I had done nothing to deserve being placed in the slammer. I was sitting there thinking, I can't wait to express my innocence! I was seated in the front of the class for all to see and hear my defense. I couldn't wait to tell that class how I had been a model citizen all my life. They needed to know that I was a professional and a true asset to Memphis. I would never hit my wife or any other woman. These people needed to know that.

Heck, I had created African American history displays for the malls, for the churches, and for the schools. I had spoken to teenagers about career goals. I had coached at St. Paul Catholic School. I was bursting at the seams to get that out there. How dare they incarcerate a man like me!

The good thing was that I was number eight in line to tell my story. The first person was a White girl that had to be about twenty-one years old. She stood and said that she was having an argument with her mom while they were traveling from the mall. She said that her mom was driving her home and pestering her about decisions that she made in her life. Suddenly, she warned her mom to "shut the hell up or she was going to knock the crap out of her!" She went on to say that her mom didn't take her threats seriously enough! Then she rolled her eyes toward the class and said that she smacked her mom a couple of times just to shut her the hell up! After her mom drove the car into an office building she was placed under arrest! "So here I am," she said.

The second person was an African American girl around twenty-five years old. She said that a female co-worker had been disrespecting her and flirting with her man. "I had that heifer on the clock," she said. "I knew it was just a matter of time before it was me and her! I finally caught that witch when she got stuck in traffic on Interstate 240. I pulled her out of her car and started whipping her butt. I kept trying to hold her still so the cars could bump her head as they went passing by!"

I was now twitching and looking around the classroom, thinking, "Oh my, I may have been safer in jail!" But it was poker face time. The third person was another African American girl around twenty-seven years old. She stood up, introduced herself, and told of her account. She said, "I knew my man was cheating and I knew I was going to catch them together!" She continued that she was driving by her man's apartment when she noticed her boyfriend hugging the woman she had suspected he was sleeping with. She said, "After recognizing the two fools I stepped on the gas pedal and drove right into their asses. Both of those son-of-dogs shot straight up in the air!"

Now I was looking around, sweating, and hoping a guard or a probation officer was nearby just in case these people had a relapse! I was saying to myself, "These students need a lot more than Anger Management!" After a few more horror stories it was my turn to stand and talk. All I was thinking was that I can't tell my Vanilla story. Not in here! I can't look like a wimp among these deviants. I would not go out like that! I only needed to complete the course. The court part was over. No way I could damage myself unless I was stupid enough to end up downtown in jail again. Nah, I had learned my lesson. So I decided to go for it!

I stood up, told my name, and I started dropping details of my arrest. I told the class "that my wife was spending my damn money without my damn permission." I even added that, "She was buying crap for other members of her damn family." I said,"I worked too damn hard for my damn dough. Then she had the audacity to get all smart mouthed about the crap too! I grabbed that dumb witch before she knew it. I went Wham Wham Wham across her damn head; then I dragged her butt through the house like a damn rag doll on a broom. I kept saying 'Witch, who money dammit, who money..." as I was smacking her "BAM BAM BAM"!. I even took two dollars out of her damn pockets which had to be my damn money also! I bet she won't touch another damn red cent of my damn money anymore."

I looked around the room and I could see the men touching their back pockets just to secure their wallets and the women were clutching their purses! I think I got through that class with flying colors.

Laughter suddenly filled the air along with sounds of choking, coughing, and smacking of the bar tables. Dylan was so overwhelmed with my lies, I even got a kick out of my story. I knew what would come next was much deeper and more intimate than any of my prior adventures. Dylan was wide-eyed like an owl that was thirsty for more vermin. So I saw an opportunity to open a different door.

Are You My Daddy??
Feeling a Presence of Me!

AS A PRESCHOOLER I picked up on conversations between Mom and Aunt Kathy regarding who my dad was. Of course, I knew many kids without fathers but it was a weird thing for me. I was so used to the madness of my mom and Aunt Kathy that the thought of someone else with idiotic ideas in my life was frightening! I would watch and listen to other kids idolizing their stray dads. I never did. Nor did I dare mention who my dad was! When I was asked I would simply say that God was my father!

Those kids would speak proudly about meetings with their dads! They even talked about the restrictions and the regimens their dads had placed upon them. It was their way of letting everyone know that they actually had a father. I really didn't see the glamour of it all! Oh, I needed discipline, direction, and a role model; but I was afraid of another parent with insane notions. I wanted a level-headed dad without the mania that Mom and Aunt Kathy made me accustomed too!

I saw my real dad at a local grocery store (Little Star) when I was around nine years old! Up until then I had no idea of what he actually looked liked. I just knew his name, which I registered in my head. I purposely walked as close as I could just to get a good look at him! He was a giant compared to the miniature-sized kid that I was. I didn't know him nor did he know me, yet I felt intimidated. I could tell he was someone in the city unlike anyone I had known except

Pastor Lloyd or Principal Shell Shock. People with status just have a way of receiving an overflow of attention.

When I took up baseball I became a decent player. I found out later that the team I played for just happened to be sponsored by my dad's church (U.M. Baptist). During my Little League years I had not a clue of the connection or the correlation. It was just pure coincidence or fate because the team existed long before I picked up a bat and glove.

Our team was mediocre even though I stood out at times. I always made sure to show up against any and all competition, regardless of the outcome. But I do remember saying to myself that I would set this park on fire if I thought my dad was watching!

I ended up having that wish fulfilled on a much bigger stage. After the season was over I was selected to rejoin my old team (BKC) that was in the playoffs against the champions of the Northside. The game would be played across from my dad's house.

Did he know who I was? I doubt it. Would he even be at the game? I wasn't sure. But I had better bring my "A" Game!

When I got to the park I was shaking like a loose leaf on a tree. There had to be about 400 people in attendance. Somehow I felt they were all there to critique me. I was as scared as I was when I first entered the sport. I was the starting 2nd baseman. With my addition I was expected to be a major link to the new team's chance of victory! My focus was completely off long before I took the field. I kept watching the crowd and not the game itself. When play began I made the first error on a routine grounder that cost our team two runs. We were getting our lunch handed to us. I wasn't even close to playing at my normal level.

My previous coach would have known that something was wrong with his star player. But such was not the case. The leader of this team had players that were much bigger, better known, and far more seasoned than myself. He had other problems beyond my mental let down.

Regardless, I needed to pull myself together. I was always a tough out in the Southside league. I had only fanned out five times that whole season. Three of those strike outs were due to silliness on my part at the plate. On this day I was facing the toughest pitcher I had batted against all season yet he wasn't even that team's best thrower! They were loaded with more talent beyond anything I had ever competed against.

There I was in the game of my life and I was stinking up the joint! Of all days I had no room for failure.

We were down 9 to zero in the 5th inning when suddenly we got two players on base. It was my turn at bat. I knew it was time to deliver the goods or forever live in shame. Suddenly, I hit a line drive that came within inches of clearing the right field fence! That shot brought all the runners home while I landed safely at second base. I had never homered in my brief career. But to me it felt like a Grand Slam! I was so ecstatic that I nearly walked off the bag while celebrating! Eventually, I would score through a steal and a pass ball. I had a hand in all three of the runs with which we ended the game! I felt like a weight had been lifted, even though we still lost the championship. Our team had only two hits for the entire game. But my two run double was the biggest! It was also the farthest hit for either team. I may not have made anyone proud but I didn't have to leave the park with my head down!

Who in the Hell Are You?

IN THE SUMMER of 1977 I was heading into my senior year of high school. I was at the Columbus Public Library just to get a few books when I noticed some ladies checking me out! I started conversing with them as much as possible. I was hoping to get lucky and win over a friend.

Out of nowhere walked in this man that was all of 6 feet 3 inches tall with an aura about him! I didn't notice his approach because I was deeply engaged in my foolish conversation.

It was my dad! It had been eight years since I first saw him. I was thinking, "OH WOW, now what? and OH WOW" once again! Ok, it was poker face time! My dad knew the ladies that I was flirting with and they knew him. They shared warm greetings and talked a bit about school. I was motionless in my seat. Poker faced perhaps but frozen to the chair! My dad walked over and said, "Who are you, young man?"

I forced a smile while thinking, "Wow and Wow again! How do I answer this?"

No doubt there was a pregnant pause while we stared at each other! Like a contestant on a T.V. game show, I looked my dad square in the eyes and I said my first, middle, and last name! My dad stumbled and took a seat across from me. My information must have smashed him like a punch to the chest! He gathered himself, then started to fire questions in rapid succession about Bennie (no surprise there), about my Aunt Kathy, and about this mystery kid that had been scarred by boiling water! I answered them all. He even asked my intentions after high school! At that point I became somewhat annoyed with his charade, so I stated, "I'm not sure what I am going to do." But there wasn't a doubt in my mind that I was going to college. I decided to play coy just like him! My dad just sat there in utter silence while looking me completely up and down. I sat there in utter silence while also looking him completely up and down. He quietly regained his strength. He then rose to his feet and walked off without saying another word. I was left sitting stone-faced and shocked! I was also trying to regain my strength while asking myself, "What the hell just happened?" For me it was as if I had come face to face with "the ghost of years past."

I found my balance and walked to the rails of the balcony. As I looked below I saw these two little cute kids with books at the checkout desk. It was the first I had ever seen them. I kept watching and taking in everything that unfolded before me. My dad would occasionally glance up but eventually he walked right out the door! I really didn't know how to feel. I say again I really didn't know how to feel except ABANDONED!

My dad didn't say a lot but it was obvious that he had some ongoing contact with my Aunt Kathy throughout the years. I knew nothing about nothing until that day! I had such an EMPTY feeling for months after that encounter! I would never speak of that moment to anyone or anybody for many years to come.

Close Enough to Touch

BEFORE I OFFICIALLY met my dad I would cross his path a few more times like a stranger in the night.

I started college the summer of 1978 at Mississippi State University. Between the summers of 1978 and 1979 I would see my dad on the steps of the College Union. I was just a face in the crowd! My dad and his associates had to have been taking classes at my university. I would walk right by him yet he never knew who I was.

In another instance I ran into my dad at a clothing store in East Columbus. I had become quite the snazzy dresser. Since I had money from my work study jobs, school loans, and college grants I was able to afford my own look. I became a blazer and khaki guy, just like the campus preppies.

As I was picking through the jackets in the men's section I saw my dad shopping for clothing as well. I immediately dashed through the racks and out of sight. I was not prepared for another sudden encounter! Once again I doubt if he saw me or if he would have even recognized me! But I was taking no chances.

I popped out of the other side of the displays only to see this pretty little girl with big gorgeous eyes standing and staring out of the store window. She had to be about thirteen years old at the time. I walked ever so near but not close enough to be noticed! I was simply curious and somewhat in awe. I wanted to speak to her but why? What was there to gain? I collected myself, returned the blazer, and headed back across the tracks.

Aiming High

DURING MY JUNIOR year in college, the world that I knew was un-raveling like a blown tire on the interstate. Even though I had fixed my car from the wreck of 1979 it was never the same. My ride had been deteriorating for some time. I didn't have the money to keep up with all of the needed repairs.

I had distanced myself from Mom and Aunt Kathy. Mom had been working her five finger deals. Aunt Kathy had turned into Quickdraw Kathy with her gun threats! Needless to say, I was not in good standing with either of them!

My grades had fallen well below my ability. I had always loved school but I didn't want it anymore. I felt alone, depressed, and scared for the first time in my life. No doubt I desperately needed a shot in the arm.

So I decided to join the Air Force like so many other guys. I took the test and I was bused to Jackson, Mississippi for the physical. The examination was a very humiliating process where I had to strip down and allow a group of doctors to examine my backside. I felt molested in front of the world. The doctors shook my hand and told me to con-tinue on even though I would have gladly taken some hush money! It was so far so good until I was asked about my burns. Ultimately, I failed the exam and I was denied entry into the U.S. military.

As I was riding back to Columbus with all the applicants, I kept thinking, "What now?" I had taken my shot and came up mighty short. I had no other cards to play! I kept hearing a voice in my head saying, "It time to meet your dad." I really, really didn't want to meet him. It wasn't time for me to meet him. And what if he didn't want to meet me! However, going back to school in my state of mind wasn't what I needed to do. It was during that ride from Jackson to Starkville when I decided to call my dad!

Let's Talk!

SO THE STAGE was set. I had to "eat crow" "punk out" and "swallow my tongue"! I was going to call my dad for what would be the shock of his life. I knew where he worked so I called him during his business hours. I got his secretary on the phone and I told her my name. She put me through to my dad. He asked me to say who was calling and I told him my name again. He said, "I beg your pardon; please repeat your name!"

It was total recall! I gave him my full name just like before! And just like in 1977 he was stunned and he was silent! He cleared his throat and told me to meet him at his school on a Saturday. Of course I agreed.

Since my car had broken down I had to walk ten miles to his office. I was desperate and was used to walking, so it was no big deal.

I was hoping for a good talk. But I honestly wanted to see where things would go. I desperately needed another car! Without it I had no semblance of life. I had no access to bigger and better jobs.

I was hopeful and feeling a relief even before our meeting. My hopes were off the charts! Life had been my burden and not my joy. I knew I also needed therapy in a bad way! But I couldn't go there. That would have been a very bad look.

I got to his school as scheduled with my preppie look. We shook hands and he led me to his work area. I was in the administrator's office, which had always been bad ju ju for yours truly! My history of office visits were populated with snapshots of Principal Shell Shock breaking boat paddles and belts on my ass! So being comfortable and confident was a struggle within itself.

As soon as I sat down the questions began. He asked what made me call? I told him it was time. Then he went through the same circus of 1977. "How's Bennie?" he said. I was like, "Wow, here we go again!" But I responded, "Bennie is ok."

Next was, "How's Aunt Kathy?" Another "wow moment" for me but I responded again with, "She's doing ok." In reality I hadn't spoken with Aunt Kathy since she threatened me with her six shooter!

This time I brought a better poker face. Our first date left me standing alone on the dance floor. I was going to anticipate all head shots and body blows this time! As I looked him over I noticed that we had the same cow eyes. It was as if I was looking at a reflective time machine! Yes, no doubt that we were related! He did stand most of the time while I sat and listened. He had all of his guard up when he really didn't have to. Even though we were alone, I felt the presence of a security team. Yet, it was just me and my nerves feeling the pressure! I was playing against the wind and I knew it. This was his turf and his ball game and he was the referee! But such was life for me. If I was going to make an impression then I had to walk a tightrope without a pole or a net.

We talked for about an hour but it felt like an entire week. Finally, he asked what I had been hoping for! He said, "How can I help you?"

I kept my composure and said, "Well, I do need another car."

He then said, "I'll see what I can do."

At that moment I felt really good! I was thinking that I might get back on track. I wasn't sure how many wishes I was to be granted. I still needed the work of a gypsy, or a soothsayer, or a village shrink just to be considered a halfway normal being.

I felt a sudden surge when he stated, "You have made my day." He continued on and added, "Shucks, you have made my year!"

I followed that with my first smile of the evening. No one had ever said that about me! No sidekick, girlfriend nor relative. He drove me home and we decided to meet again when I came back from college. At that point I was excited. I saw my life taking a new shape. I could hope for a real family! I could hope for someone to talk to and maybe a dollar to line my pockets.

I felt Dylan clutching my shoulder in support! He knew I was in floundering in the deep end better than I did! I heard him say, "Go slow, young man! Go slow..." However, I thought I was holding up pretty good. I was kinda worried about Dylan. So I passed him a fresh beach towel and I asked if I should go on. He gave me a head nod. So I pushed onward!

Car-Jacked by Aunt Kathy

ON THE FOLLOWING weekend, Dad picked me up from home and took me to his office. As I walked in I was looking around for souvenirs like leather belts, shop made paddles, or cattle prods. I didn't see any so I sensed the coast was clear! He then told me that he had spoken with Aunt Kathy. Immediately, I turned on the poker face because only evil and ignorance came out of that woman. I was 21 years old! A man! Why in the hell would he talk to that nimrod? Yet I understood. Aunt Kathy was part of my inner circle and it was wise to talk to someone that knew me best. However, I knew there would be crap in the air. If Aunt Kathy was involved then loose particles of crap were soon to follow! I was just holding on while reaching for my breathing apparatus. Then it happened. He said, "Aunt Kathy stated that she wouldn't get me a car if it was entirely up to her." I almost sank through the floor! I knew she wanted to hurt me but that was brain surgery with a sling blade. Dad was attempting to make a connection. So for me to show anger or disrespect would have been "The kiss of death!" I just had to sit there and take it! Aunt Kathy should have demanded that Dad buy me two or three cars, a couple of bicycles, and a bus pass! How dare she step on me like that? The both of them had me over a barrel. I had to accept defeat or find another way. Sadly, my nearest and dearest relative had finally gotten even! Once again I was foolish enough to underestimate my Aunt Kathy.

Me: The Lion Tamer!

THE FIRST PART of my plan was to face the lion and look for an opening. I had to go to Aunt Kathy and find out where I stood. I couldn't believe the monster she had made me out to be! Understandably, she was amused to see me crawling back but that was my only card.

She was very dismissive and certainly indignant at first. She had a relaxed, devious, and smug look about her. It was obvious that she had been expecting me. But I was there to listen so listen was what I did. She was choosing her words as if they were scripted or well planned out.

She mentioned nothing about dad buying me a car. That was no surprise to me. She had me where she wanted me. She was even gloating! Yet I stayed focused and above it all. I made sure to overlook all of her smirks. I knew I was her 2nd placed nephew! But I wanted her to see me as the little nephew she used to know!

Suddenly, she began to soften. She transferred her resentments off of me and onto my dad. Amazing how she operated. There had to be a good and there had to be an evil. She would tell me that dad invited her out to his office. She went on to say, "I cursed him the hell out when I got there! I went up one wall and down another one." I had no idea as to why nor did I ask. I was an adult! I was concerned about the now. So if she was grandstanding or displacing blame as to defend me or to impress me I really didn't care! I cared less about scoring points or paybacks. But here's the thing. I had never inferred or asked my mom "Who is my dad?" all of my life! I had never asked my Aunt Kathy "What can you tell me about my dad?" I just happened to pick up who my dad was at an early age! So I accepted that I was father-less, just like I accepted that I was poor.

Like any rebellious kid I loved the fact I could do whatever I want-ed and whenever I wanted too! Unfortunately, I had no money to go with that autonomy. I came to cherish being able to come and go as I so pleased. Yet I hated the reality that I had no support, no direction, no love, and no role models. I was at a point where I really needed a reliable voice to talk to. I needed a mentor in the worst kind of way!

My future was at stake. That was my only concern. Aunt Kathy gave me a hug and a smile, then off I went into the great unknown. I was more uncertain than ever before. I'm sure her affections were dis-ingenuous at best. Yet I was still ok with that. I wasn't there to beg her for her love or for her help! I just wanted to feel her out. I was on full damage control. Whatever happened after that, then so shall it be!

Otherwise, disappearing out of sight, leaving Columbus, and dropping out of Mississippi State University was my Plan B. The clock was definitely ticking!

Dinner at 2:00 PM

DAD INVITED ME out to meet the family. I really didn't see that coming! It was like getting a job after a failed interview! First of all, I was butchered by Aunt Kathy. She was "the Christian of The South Side." She was the guardian. She was the go-to person when it came to me. Of course, my score from her was a definite "two thumbs down." Secondly, I knew Dad had to be concerned about my past and my associations. Even I knew that would be treacherous waters for me. I was from the Trash Alley. That was my community. I knew people from "the Catfish Alley" like I knew my teachers. I hung out with thugs from the Frog Bottom, the Burns Bottoms, the Red Line, the S-Curve, the Sandfield, the Morning Side, and places that shall remain nameless. I even knew all of the "Legends of the Hood." There were Sin Man, Swap, Boo Boo, Emp-Man, Cookie Man, Shank, Polar Bear, Bae Willy, Bae Bruh, Skullhead Ned, Pimp, Crunch, and Goat Turd just to name a few. I was thinking maybe Dad needed me for "show and tell" for the kids in his neighborhood! I was going to be the hardliner to scare those wayward suburban brats back into reality. Third, the people in my community never invited anyone over for breakfast, lunch, or dinner. I mean never! And especially yours truly! If you got invited over to eat then it was all part of a grand scheme to embarrass or to humiliate you.

I was no way prepared to meet my dad's family. I was totally out of my element. However, Dad had planned to pick me up at 2:00 p.m. on a Sunday afternoon. I needed a spiritual intervention. So I headed off to church before our dinner rendezvous. I was hoping that

Pastor Lloyd could work some magic for a troubled wretch like me!

As I entered the church I was shaking like the dope-man in the wrong place with the wrong package. Standing next to a stained glass window was Teddy Charles! He was the lead usher. His job was to balance the placement of parishioners throughout the church. Teddy Charles. guided me toward the front of the church but I ducked away to a different opening. I wasn't falling for another one man crucifixion! I ended up sitting next to Sexy Patty. I wasn't trying to hit on her. I needed the Hands of God and not a girlfriend! I took the first available seat as immediate cover. It had been awhile since I'd been there. I wanted to fit in as quickly and as quietly as possible. Since I had my own issues, I failed to noticed that Sexy Patty was already clenching a napkin and sweating profusely from head to toe. Nonetheless, she looked hotter than a fever!

The choir stood up and Aunt Kathy led them in her own rendition of Leaning on the Everlasting Arms. Singing backup were the twins, Mary and Martha, with identical hats. They sounded as bad as Aunt Kathy but I wasn't going to be the one to say that. I never really liked that song but it was sweet and divine for that moment. Even Sexy Patty looked over and smiled at me! She had a smile that could melt cold butter. Her stare nearly caused me to make a hymn request. "I feel the FIRE BURNING in my HEART" would have been my selection but I quickly returned to my hour of need. I was there to be an instrument of the Word. There had to be a sign for me.

Pastor Lloyd took to the podium and asked the congregation to open their Bibles to Matthew 8:23-27. He preached about Jesus calming the waters on the lake. Pastor Lloyd shouted again and again, "Peace be still, Peace be Still" as Jesus commanded in the Bible. I felt my own nerves coming to a rest. Out of nowhere Sexy Patty would squeeze my hand with everything she had! I gleamed her way, thinking that she was hitting on me! What a blessing that would have been. But that was not to be. Sexy Patty had gotten touched by the Holy Spirit"! She threw her hands in the air to wave at Jesus and my hand went up too. A member behind me held my shoulders and said, "Son,

It's going to be all right." Apparently, Sexy Patty didn't get the same encouragement that I had received She lurched out of her seat to shout and dance yet still locked digit to digit with me. I had no choice but to rise with her. Her stomping helped to drive the heels of her stilettos straight through my canvas shoes. I started to shout in pain while hopping on one leg. I blurted out, "Jesus, Oh Jesus!" She danced and shouted to the East while I screamed and hopped to the West! I had planned to go unnoticed. But it was too late! Everyone could see that old heathen was back amongst them. And if that wasn't enough they were so moved by my expressions of "the Holy Spirit" that a whole section of worshipers got up to hop on one leg too! I had a Soul Train line bouncing up and down behind me screaming, "Jesus, Oh Jesus"!

Eventually, Teddy Charles and the ushers would get to me. In so many ways I knew Teddy Charles enjoyed seeing my spiritual outbursts. He and the others took me to a quiet area of the church. They took turns wiping away my tears of pain. It was amazing how they all wanted to touch me just to feel, "the Power of the Lord" They even tried to coach me on how to handle "the Holy Spirit." They said that, "You have to be careful when the Word touches you!" Next, they gave me Sexy Patty's lone stiletto. She had already left the church. They had assumed that she was my girl. No doubt she was the angel of Zion Union church until she crucified her neighbor.

There I was sitting in pain, caressing my foot, and holding Sexy Patty's stiletto pump. I suddenly had a Cinderella moment! But with my luck she would damage my other foot as I tried to return her missing shoe! Fortunately, my pain brought me back to my senses. Sexy Patty had already inflicted more agony than I cared to handle. I quickly dropped all notion of seeing her again.

In the meantime all the faithfuls came by to say, "Praise the Lord" and "Just trust in God!" Even Aunt Kathy showed up to say, "Bless you, baby." Finally, Pastor Lloyd stopped by to thank me for stirring the congregation. He stroked my head and said, "God is Good!" I replied, "All the time." I knew then that I was ready for dinner!

Church had come to a close. I needed to get back home. I didn't want Dad waiting on me so I picked up my pace. I walked into Bennie who was staggering in the opposite direction. I stopped and asked, "Where are you going?"

He said, "I hear that the church is breaking the wine today."

I told him, "Yes, but COMMUNION is at six o'clock p.m.! You are way too early."

He then asked, "Will they have wine during COMMOTION?"

I responded with, "Yes, but it's called Communion! Why don't I walk you home, then you can come back later for your blessing!"

Bennie replied, "I don't need the blessing; I just need them to pass me the bottle."

I didn't have the heart to tell him that he would only get a miniature sized glass of wine.

As Dad drove out to his house everything became a fable. We practically disappeared into the woods. He opened the door to his home and I stepped on a cloud. I had never experienced so much tranquility in a house! The silence was deafening. I wanted to make a run for it. There had to be something sinister at play. Everyone was so nice and cordial. That never happened when I was around. I kept looking for an escape hatch just in case I was in the wrong dimension. I checked the walls for signs of Ghosts, Devils, Dead Dogs, and Haints. I saw no remnants nor did I hear any voices. The coast was clear. But I chose not to eat with the family just in case a setup was in play.

The family invited me to stay for the big sleepover. That was a bigger challenge than they could have imagined. I had to bring my own recordings of shooting, stabbing, break-ins, robberies, cussing, fighting, door slamming, cars screeching, gambling, and sirens just to get into a sleep mode. After that I slept like a baby in a manger!

Slowly, that serenity began to soak into my bones. Unbeknownst to everyone, the healing had begun!

Dad did buy me a car. It was a giant step forward. But I always felt as if he was playing prevent defense against me. He was always so guarded.

I found it odd that he never asked me about my mom. I wasn't looking for answers, nor was I stupidly wanting them to get together. I just wanted an opening to talk about my relationship with my mom! Unfortunately, that door would never budge in the slightest! However, I cherished all of my visits with the family. I would sit motionless for hours while trying to rub that peace all over my face!

How Do You Say Goodbye?

SHORTLY AFTER I started my career with the FAA I met my kids' mother. We had our first kid out of wedlock. The thought of me being an irresponsible parent was the only vision Dad had of me! I was not ready for marriage. The stresses of the job and the work environment kept me on edge. Terminations were a daily occurrence. I didn't want to blow my big chance after giving my all just to get there! I was disappointed about how Dad saw me and more disappointed at how he saw my little princess. I was a big boy! I could handle his denial of me but no one was going to treat my little girl as less than. Our would-be relationship was unraveling at warp speed.

I decided to handwrite a letter surmising my history of him and me. In my letter I told him that I was stepping away from his world and that I was sorry for the intrusion! I took the letter to a secretarial service. They remade the letter without correcting any of my grammatical errors. I stood there trying to proofread the typed pages while I sensed tears of sheer frustration. That office came to a standstill watching me in full melt down! I dashed into the restroom to gather myself while protecting the pages from further smears. It was tough but it was certainly time to move on!

I got a call from Dad in the spring of 2003. He said he wanted to see me. It had been five years since we last talked. I was living in Houston, Texas. He was a 12-hour drive away. I told him that I would see him around Thanksgiving of that year. I never made it in time. Dad passed away in October. We would never get that talk.

I got the family together and we headed to Dad's burial. I was still bitter but it was a time for closure and respect. I held strong from the news of Dad's passing. I was gaining more strength as his funeral drew near. But irony breaks suckers every day. At his memorial I was the emotional bastard that couldn't get it together! As tough as I wanted to be I couldn't fight back my tears. All the things that were lost came bubbling out and over the top! Such events as: We never went fishing! We never had a road trip! We never had a beer! We never went to "The Game"! The list was far too deep and far too long! But beyond that vacuum of "What If" and "Only If" I lost his calming force and his voice of reason forever!

As I looked up, Dylan was kicking sand and staring away from me! I didn't mind his lack of focus. The evening clouds had cast a badly needed shadow. Dylan was speechless and so was I. We needed a moment just to reset. I covered my head as my masseuse hacked away at my new found tension. Dylan also decided to step away and call his kids!

After getting karate chops to the neck and an elbow to the back I was perked and ready to move on. Suddenly, Dylan laid down his drink, sat up Indian style, then told me to pick him up again. I asked him, "What do you mean"?

He said, "Make me smile again!"

I raised my eyebrows, gave him a wink, and said, "Sure, I think I can do that. So listen up…"

The Search for Our Friends!

I GRABBED A jacket and a flashlight from my room. Without it our rescue would have been futile. It was sheer darkness. The whole lot was far from anything I could have imagined. I felt like I was navigating Mars or some deserted land. It was like walking through a landfill or a junkyard at night with minimal lighting. Every step had to be made with caution. We generally knew the perimeter quite well, but it was all foreign at that point.

Words had spread that two more of our workers were missing. That made four people unaccounted for! One was a female named Dale that was barricaded in her room. Charlotte and Mack were reportedly trapped at the bar. Finally, Derrick was last known to be at the gym.

We went for Dale first. When we got to her room we could hear the moans and screams of hysteria. She was calling for help with the little energy she had left. We tried to kick her door open but there was no movement. Too many items had jammed the entry way. However, she had some luck. She resided on the first floor so we climbed in through the window. Dale was lying on the floor covered under everything imaginable. There was a table on top of her. A dresser rested on top of the table. Dust, glass, molding, and a 40 inch T.V. added to her restraints. She was experiencing severe back pain. It wasn't wise to move her. So we cleared away as much debris as possible. Then we made a passage through to the door. The nurse wanted Dale taken to the military hospital. The roads were impassable for the average vehicle. Dale would have to be carried on foot. The hospital was about six miles away from us. Our camp wasn't safe at all but the outside was far more risky! Yet Dale needed immediate medical attention.

We got four other volunteers to take Dale to the entrance of the military base on a stretcher. They made it to the gate and back safely.

Next, we went after Charlotte and Mack. Miraculously, Charlotte was able to escape the bar with only cuts and scrapes. We found her standing where the bar once stood. She looked as if she was waiting on a taxi! She was so badly shaken that she hardly said a word. The building that once held the bar was completely obliterated. Charlotte would later tell us that she was serving drinks to Mack then suddenly without notice she found herself standing alone on the outside!

We knew we had to get Charlotte to the panic room for further observation. In the interim she murmured that Mack was someplace in the bar. We needed to get to him. We called out for Mack. He called back faintly in return. That was a good sign! We pushed through the rubble only to find Mack sitting on a stool where our watering hole used to be. He was eerily sitting there while waiting on his third order of Jack and Coke!

Mack stated, "My back is out and I lost my glasses." We kept talking to Mack in order to keep him calm. He told us, "I was sitting at the bar with Charlotte when suddenly the floor disappeared. I hurt my back while climbing onto my seat. In the process I lost my glasses and my liquor shot of Jack!"

Our nurse wanted Mack moved to the military hospital as well. However, Mack was 6 feet 2 inches tall plus 240 pounds. He would have to be carried by stretcher to the entrance of the base just like Dale. That was a tall order by any standards. I was not going to volunteer for that job unless I was Mack's last hope! Luckily for Mack the same gurney crew agreed to take him to the foot of the base.

Dylan was quiet but very attentive. He asked me what I was thinking during those moments. I said, "Dylan, adrenaline was holding me up! Otherwise, I would have been too exhausted to continue! I had been involved in many hustles and work details but none as death defying as that night. While I was preparing for our final rescue I had residual thoughts of previous jobs shooting through my head."

Man for the Jobs: Stealing Time

AFTER SEEING OTHER kids with toys that I didn't have, I learned to hustle by running errands, picking fruit, or doing lawn care. I started when I was eight years old. I would buy toys like G.I. Joe, Hot Tracks, and Rock-em-Sock-em. Those items did make me feel normal for that stage of my life! But I had to put in a lot of time and a lot of hard work to get what I wanted.

I saw this watch in a local department store that I wanted very badly. So I made it my target and saved all my money to get that watch. I went into overdrive. I ran errand after errand. I doubled my load of picking fruit. I raked leaves and cut hedges like a kid possessed. Eventually, I was able to buy my fourteen dollar Timex watch. I was so proud of myself.

I only got to show it off just once! On that day I was stopped on the side of our house by this thug called Goat Turd. This guy was about fifteen years old and a constant terror in the community. He asked me what time it was. I peered at my Timex while keeping my distance and told him the time. He then said that he had to see the actual time. I held my arm so he could see my watch, then I quickly dropped my hand down to my side. Goat Turd protested that he didn't get to see the "real time."

I told him, "Yes you did" as I tried to make my way to the house. He grabbed me and suspended me in the air while trying to remove my Timex! I was kicking and screaming, yet keeping a death grip on my watch. He suddenly bit into my wrist until I could no longer take the pain! So I screamed and said, "Take it. Take it!" He unbuckled my watch band and immediately disappeared out of sight I ran inside wailing and shouting but there was no one at home to help me! I wanted the police in the worst way. We had no phone! I ran to the neighbor's house where I would call the Columbus Police department.

The police came out and asked me to identify my assailant. I knew exactly where Goat Turd lived. The cops put me in the cruiser and took me directly to his house. I walked inside, escorted by the officers. In the back of the house was Goat Turd. He was now wearing my Timex as his own fashion statement. My description had been so spot on that the cops never considered Goat Turd's defense. He was handcuffed and led out of the house. He kept staring at me in anger. I smiled at him and said, "Where you are going you won't need to keep time." He sneered at me while the cops laughed back at him. I ended up having to walk back to my house. I had gotten my watch back but Goat Turd stole my transportation in the end!

The Carnival Mice

ONCE I GOT around the age of ten I expanded to different jobs. I was mowing lawns for those who had a lawn mower but were either too lazy or too old to do it themselves. I had quite a list of customers that needed my services. I was buying tobacco, snuff, cigarettes, and groceries for my clients. I was very reliable regardless of rain, shine, sleet, or snow! My people would recommend me to others because I was so good at my job. However, my business took a major hit because of two grave mistakes on my part.

My closest friend, Walter, noticed that I was never broke. He wanted to know what I was doing to get my money. I actually had more errands than I could handle so I gave him a few names to help him out. That was my first mistake! Walter started to break into my routine and my money!

Secondly, I had a client named Mrs. Sally that had me on a four day rotation. I would buy her snuff tobacco like clockwork. However, the carnival had come to town on the previous weekend, and I won twelve dollars betting on the mice. Of course, that was more money than I had been making on my errands. The carnival was between the store and Mrs. Sally's house. I figured I would drop in and play the mice in between stops. Unbeknownst to me Walter went to Mrs. Sally's house right behind my back! I was running about twenty minutes later than normal. I left the carnival to resume my duties when I met Walter striding toward me with anger and attitude! He told me that Mrs. Sally had sent him out to look for me because she feared I had stolen her two dollars! She also instructed Walter to "catch me, get her money, and beat the snot out of me!" Needless to say, Mrs. Sally was off my client list after that.

The Glitz Cafe

MY MOM WORKED at The Glitz cafe in downtown Columbus. She would bus tables and keep the place clean. They needed an extra hand so Mom recommended me for the job. I gladly took the position. The problem was the long hours during school and work during the summer months. Baseball had occupied my past two summers.

My duties were short orders, busing tables, and keeping the place clean. I actually enjoyed that job for some time. I even took another job in Catfish Alley, the rough section of town as the cleaning guy. I had money all the time but I didn't spend it wisely. I would go to the movies every weekend while splurging on fast food. It was the first time that I could afford hamburgers, hotdogs, French fries, and ice cream. It was too easy for me to spend my money. I had never experienced those treats outside of the school cafeteria. But it felt so good for the time being!

The owners of The Glitz cafe were very nice to Mom and me. The big boss had this Studabaker sedan in perfect condition. I would gawk and circle his car in awe almost every day. The big boss was also the top chef. He cooked on special days and also on the weekends. Otherwise, I would do the hamburgers, fried eggs, or toast during the week. I gained an ear and appreciation for Country music because that was all they played on the juke box.

One day I was cooking and busing tables when this customer (around 30 years old) called me a Nigger just after I delivered his food! I stood there and looked at him for quite awhile. I was completely knocked out of my shoes. All of the customers appeared to

181

have liked me before that. My meals were always timely and prepared as requested. I had so many negative thoughts running through
my head. I had always viewed bullies as being attention getters, in-
secure, and deviously minded people! There I was sizing this guy up
with the same characterizations and then some! I couldn't help but
think 'why would this older man pick on a kid?' I had lived in a completely African American community all my life and I had never been
called a Nigger by a White person. Yes, African American people said
that word many times around me but the sting was not even close
to what I was feeling! Even when Mississippi was completely segregated I had interactions with Whites and I had never been assaulted
with that word. One of the owners came over to remove me from the
scene. The boss scolded the customer while I returned to the kitchen.
It was obvious that she knew this guy because they were on a first
name basis. It wasn't the owner's fault but I felt so humiliated! I really
couldn't face her after that incident.

That event killed my joy of working there! I was stupid to let
that moment effect my income but I was twelve and I thought like a
twelve-year-old! Eventually, I would be fired for too many no-shows
and constant tardiness. The money from The Glitz Cafe meant very
little to me after that.

As strange as it may sound, my termination was like a release
from my mental bondage!

One Butt Shine Coming Up!

AFTER THE GLITZ Cafe I didn't work very much. I found stimulation and refuge with being a team trainer with the Caldwell High School football team. It was just a different cover that allowed me to escape home and the stresses of life. I didn't want the everyday commitment of work at the age of thirteen. Luckily, I could find a hustle here and there that would bring me money.

One of the jobs I found was Fred's Car Wash on Highway 82 (Main Street). I had to get up early on Saturday to make the selection of washers. We would service all the cars by hand. If I made the cut I could make $15 to $20 for that day. Cars were continuously washed with temperatures well into the 40 degree range. The more cars the better!

I had this old lady drive up in her shiny new Cadillac that really didn't need washing. However, we would turn down no customers. She told me that she wanted her car completely detailed (washed, waxed, etc.) and to make sure to wash the undercarriage. It was a very cold day so I wanted to get her car washed and cleaned as quickly as possible. I had heat on my mind! Being somewhat surprised and tickled I told the lady, "Ma'am, no one will be looking under your car." I really should have known her mindset before I opened my big fat mouth! She went on to tell me, "Son, no one is looking at my butt but I wash it anyway!" I smiled back at her and said, "One undercarriage cleaning coming right up."

Soda Waters -N- Soda Pops

THE BIGGEST OF my hustles were selling Soda Water -N- Soda Pops at Mississippi State football and basketball games. The university is located in Starkville, Mississippi which had only one soda distributor at the time.

I'd get up at dawn on the weekend and walk twelve miles to be in line for their selections. What was sad was that I was the top seller almost every time yet I had to pray that I made the cut.

I got to see a lot of top athletes such as Jim Kelly, Ray Guy, Rocky Felker, and Walter Packer. I saw some big time basketball and big time entertainment like The Harlem Globetrotters with Meadowlark Lemon and Curly Neal all for free.

But I cared less about the games or the stars! I needed money so that was my focus.

I would make $200 to $250 in one day. That was well worth getting up for. The company would give out bonuses to the top seller. That was all the motivation it took. However, I just needed a formula to pull it off. I noticed that whenever I walked between the rows (especially the fraternity sections) I was selling the drinks well before I reached the other side. It turned out that the people on those rows were buying the sodas just to get rid of me. They would even make others around them join in just so I wouldn't enter their section spilling ice, syrup, and liquids all over their well pressed outfits! Once I picked that up, then it was on! I didn't care about the insults. I was off loading racks after racks of sodas like hot cakes. Too bad the football team only played three home games a year.

Show Me Some Love

I WRECKED MY Ford Torino in the summer of my sophomore year at Mississippi State University. Not only did I damage my car, but I also severely crippled my friend, Jerry Pharr's, vehicle. I lost my everyday transportation and a good friend as well. I was completely devastated. Without a car to get around I had no circle of friends or any means of being viable. I stayed on campus more than I wanted. But it was my only way of making enough money from work-study just to repair my car. My classes were no longer my focus and my grades showed it. I just couldn't handle being unable to move around whenever I needed to!

I did everything from being an intramural referee to organizing books at the library. I worked long hours because the pay was meager at best.

A lot of hot co-eds would come in and out of the library. I was depressed but not blind! There was this girl named Valerie who would flirt with me whenever she came into the library to study or to return a book. I was trying my best to be her only friend. I happened to notice a co-worker named Marcus keeping Valerie company more than I cared for. But hey, if I noticed that Valerie was hot, then I shouldn't have been surprised that other guys noticed it too.

Marcus was a little shorter than me but he had a much bigger frame. He had a physique like a bodybuilder. I viewed him as an ex-athlete. We would converse occasionally but to me he was the competition.

One Sunday night after Marcus and me had finished our shifts, he invited me out for a joy ride around Starkville. There was not a lot to see or anything I hadn't seen before but I was certainly bored of my work routines. We talked quite a bit. He also delivered the disappointing news that Valerie already had a boyfriend. "Oh damn!" I thought. He confessed that he had known her for some time but, no, he was not the boyfriend. At that point my evening turned into a total loss.

After Marcus told me that Valerie was taken I was silently curious why he didn't show any disappointment like myself! After all, Valerie was cute, charming, sexy, and smart. How could he not feel the let down? I understood that you win some and you lose some and the world keeps on turning but that was quite a blow!

Unexpectedly, Marcus told me that he was stopping to pick up his roommate, Jackie, who worked at a local hotel. "No problem," I said. After Jackie got in the car we headed back to campus. Jackie was extremely friendly and quite a talker. I had seen Jackie around campus, but we had never met. They invited me up for a beer and a game of cards. After hearing that my chances with Valerie were out of reach I did need a moment in order to reset. I said, "Sure, I'll come up for a drink with you guys." It appeared that I was making new friends. Those new friendships set off a startling twist of events all within the matter of hours.

My roommate was back in Columbus. He would show up on Mondays for school then return home on the weekends. He was definitely a "man's man"! He was kind of a square but very focused and driven as a student. He was religious and a good role model even at his age.

A couple weeks earlier my roommate had been burning the midnight oil while playing cards with our resident assistant (RA). They would play from dusk to dawn. My roomie told me that on his final night with the RA he was presented a coin that had a penis on one side and a butt on the opposite! The RA supposedly asked my roomie "What will it be?" I couldn't stop laughing at my roommate. He didn't think it was very funny but I was doubled over in pain! No, I didn't ask what was his decision. But he walked out of the room because I couldn't keep a dry eye with him around.

So Marcus, Jackie, and me were sitting at our makeshift table playing cards and having a couple of beers. I was situated furthest from the door. We must have talked about everything that came to our minds. Unbeknownst to them I was still quietly licking my wounds from being dissed by Valerie.

Out of nowhere Marcus asked me if I thought Jackie was cute! I thought that was an odd question. The guys I knew didn't talk that way. I told Marcus "Jackie seems cool. I'm sure he gets his share of the girls."

Then Jackie asked me, "Could you like a guy like me?"

It was my Oh Crap moment. I knew then exactly what time it was!

I replied, "I think you would be a good friend," as I was getting up from the table. Suddenly Jackie attempted to pull down his pants! Now my voice was near a shouting pitch! I said, "Dude, Dude, what the hell are you doing? Get your stuff back on!"

I was wedged in the room between the table and their bed. I started moving the objects, tossing chairs, and kicking debris in order to make myself a path out of their room! Since Jackie was opposite of me, he immediately tried to cut me off at the door! As I got closer to the exit, Jackie smiled at me and said, "Just give me a hug." I tensed up in combat mode and I told Jackie, "You have less than a second to get your ass out of my way!"

Jackie moved and I rushed back to my room. I was completely rocked by what had just happened! That was definitely karma for my roommate. So I never told him anything about my evening with Marcus and Jackie!

What "Brown" Did for Me

WHILE I WAS at Jackson State University it didn't take long to realize that I needed an off campus job real bad. My roommate, Larry Battle, was working with Universal Postage (U-P). Through luck, patience, and connections, Larry got what was a rare opportunity to work there. He was also an ex-football player that made him better suited for the rigors of package handling. The company would seek out college students for their entry level positions. The work was hard, tough, part time, but with good pay and benefits.

It was a challenge just to get an interview with U-P. They would randomly make their selections from area colleges around Jackson, Mississippi. At the time JSU appeared out of the rotation. No student had been interviewed for months. I didn't want to take any chances. So I drove out to the placement offices of the other schools and put my name on their lists. As I expected, I received a call within days. I passed the interview and off to work I went.

I should have known that the process was far too easy for the money they were shelling out! My first night I was instructed to un- load boxes from the bed of an 18-wheeler with temperatures north of 100 degrees at a rate of 1300 packages per minute. Being new to the game it didn't take long for me to dehydrate and fizzle out. I had never worked so hard in such a short interval in my life! Needless to say I lasted about one hour and twenty minutes that night. The shift was four hours non-stop. I had cheated the company out of two hours forty minutes. I stumbled out of the warehouse toward my car. I ached in places that I didn't know I had. Larry was having too much fun watching me stumbling and falling on my face. I was so fatigued that I sat on the ground against my car for thirty minutes before trying to drive off the lot. Once I got home I called my girlfriend over to walk on my back until I fell asleep. If I was going to keep that job, I needed to up my game.

Someone forgot to tell Larry and U-P that there was NO QUIT in me! Two months later I was officially employed and one of the top unloaders, even though I was the smallest of the crew. One year later U-P tried to encourage me to join their management team. However, I was still in college with other ideas. I had met a recruiter named John Burkett from the Federal Aviation Administration (FAA) and he had persuaded me to try a career in Air Traffic Control. I was determined to take that apprenticeship with the FAA. I had to see if there was a mutual fit.

However, I gained exponentially from the U-P benefits. The company insurance paid the initial fee on braces for my teeth. I got surgery for my burn scars. And the company held a slot for me as I took the apprenticeship with the FAA. I had given my all just to get on board with U-P and it had returned with life-altering dividends.

My friend, Dylan, was now looking at me like a proud big brother! I said to him "Not yet, Dylan!" He said, " What do you mean"?

I told him, "I haven't gotten to Thailand yet, but I was on my way." He gave me that glazed drunken gaze so I just kept talking.

The Big Interview

AFTER GETTING SELECTED for an apprenticeship with the FAA I had to do my official interview at the Jackson International Airport (Medgar Evers Field). I didn't have a business suit but I put together a very nice ensemble that was sure to pass. I got to the place on time and sat down with the chief of Medgar Evers Airport. He showed me the layout of the FAA Air Traffic Control system. He also informed me that I had not been assigned my official work facility. All information was good as far as I was concerned. I just wanted a job. However, I had no idea what Air Traffic Controllers actually did. I just figured I would figure it out and make the adjustments.

Then he told me about the work environment. He said that many employees have very little tact or past interactions with minorities. My gleaming eyes were dimming because I could sense something problematic was unfolding.

The chief went on to give me an example of what he called cultural ignorance: He said, "I was at a Christmas party with African Americans when I requested some more NIGGER Toes!"

I was trying to hold my poker face but I had never heard the slur before. The chief stared at me for a reaction and I stared back at him, trying to decode the term! After a moment of silence, I conceded that it was a term with which I wasn't familiar. He told me that the term was used for Brazil nuts. He then confessed that it was the only racial term he had ever used. I just shook my head because obviously I was in a whole new arena.

The chief said, "I have another example for you."

I sat up, cleared my throat, and said, "Ok, go ahead."

He said, "A lot of those guys (of course he meant Whites) are down home Southerners. They use the term 'Coon-Ass' a lot!" He went on to say that they call each other that insult without thinking, but they are not being racial! Horrified, I locked eyes with him again, trying to find that poker face of mine. As I gathered myself I repeated, "COON-Ass huh?"

He nodded affirmatively. Then he told me the term was used to describe a backward redneck. Now I nodded my head as if I understood but his explanation had dropped another analogy (Backward Redneck) that I hadn't ever heard of! I was like, "Wow, that's an oxymoron for you. Could it be such a thing?" The last one he laid on me would poison my acceptance of a popular used acronym. He said, "You may hear FNG quite a bit."

Perplexed, I stared back at the chief once again. Then I asked, "What's that?"

Without hesitation he rolled out the words "Freaking NIGGER."

I was nearly knocked out of my seat but I held firm! I'm sure my heart skipped a beat but I was maintaining. I kept asking myself, "What year is this again? Are people really like that? Am I sure I want to venture into this?"

As much as my head was spinning I kept my smooth poker face! I accepted right then and right there that, "Such was the world that I lived in, so I had better toughen up!" Finally, I responded to the chief with "Wow, oh Wow!"

He nodded in the affirmative once more. I knew he would looking for something with more depth. I reached within and I said, "Sir I have been around White people all my life. Yes, I have hit some rough patches from time to time but I can cope with anyone!"

The Chief smiled back and said, "Welcome to the FAA!"

As I left the airport I felt completely flushed and drained by the things I had just learned! I wasn't into liquor but I needed a prayer and a drink if I was going to accept that job. My demeanor must have impressed the chief because shortly thereafter I was assigned to the deep south Memphis Air Route Traffic Control Center.

Memphis Center

I DON'T THINK anything can fully prepare you for raw prejudice! I had faced intimidation many times before but racism is a special kind of bullying. If a minority is of a dark complexion then there is no hiding. It is like a deer playing opossum with a wolf! If you are on the menu then that trick won't work.

It didn't matter how professional or how cordial I was, I was not welcome. It wasn't long before I was either on edge or I was trying to decipher someone's intentions.

I started out dispersing flight plans (information about the airplane destination) to the different work sectors. In between deliveries I was asked if I liked the job better than picking cotton! Being that I had never picked cotton before I had nothing with which to compare! But I had learned to just go with it. So I said, "Of course!"

A lot of other things went on that were far more of a challenge than in any place I had worked. To say I was jumpy was an understatement. Yet, if I was going to make it, then I had to pick my battles.

There were many customs and quirks that I had to observe and learn! One supervisor told me that, "Being an Air Traffic Controller was better than carrying a gun." Completely rattled, I stopped and stared at that supervisor, hoping for some clarification! He went on to explain that the guy he was training was an ex-police officer. I was deeply relieved that he went into those details!

I was a conscientious and daily reader of newspapers. I would bring the Commercial Appeal and the USA Today to work. One morning I placed my papers on the dining table, then proceeded to get my breakfast. After I returned, most of my papers were gone! I was like "What the Hell?" Come to find out that was a practice that the controllers would freely take a section of paper that you weren't currently reading. That was another tradition I learned right there "on the job."

To be an Air Traffic Controller you had to have the aptitude, the vision, the courage, and the confidence beating in your veins around the clock. Most controllers are "Type A" personalities with the arrogance of a fighter pilot. But being a minority, you had to be polite and political just to get a shot!

Air traffic controlling is not a job that is easily picked up without military experience.

I was the net zero apprentice. I was dealing with the big bully that didn't care to play ball with me. My crew supervisor didn't call me by name for two years. He would tell my trainers to "Take him to that sector," or "You train that guy," or "How's that fella doing?" I really didn't care if he talked to me or not. I didn't care if he called my name. I just wanted the job. And above all I wanted a fair chance to prove myself!

Bullies are intimidating. I had dealt with that many times before.

Bullies are territorial. I was the outsider. A bully will ignore you. I needed them to engage me if I was going to learn their craft.

Most bullies are not that cunning but these guys were. If I was going to break in, then I had to beat them at their own game.

One night I had what I thought was a small run-in with a slew of controllers on the midnight shift. They were using racial epithets that I found highly offensive so I told the supervisor on duty to just have them move their conversations to another area away from my ears. By sunrise they had turned the story on me! They were accusing me of being a militant and calling them racists.

I left work in a rage and a disgusted mood that stayed with me for hours. I tried to drive to Houston, Texas for a weekend hangout with my college roommate. After traveling for six hours I decided to refuel in Denham Springs, Louisiana. While I was at the gas pump I thought I heard the attendant shouting "Boy, you need to hang up the pump"!

I was thinking, "I can't be hearing what I think I'm hearing." The voice was that of a male who continued shouting, "Boy, you need to hang up the pump!"

Not only had I not refueled, I was now more pissed that someone would call me a "Boy?" My work encounter, along with that, "Boy" statement put me at my tipping point! I thought that was just too bold and too insulting. This was just an ass-kicking I had to take! I marched to the entry of the convenience store with anger and determination! I kicked the door open, and yelled, "I don't know who the hell yawl think you are screwing with."

There were about seven customers in line. Conversations fell to utter silence. All eyes were on this "raving Lunatic standing in the doorway!" Suddenly, a very small White lady at the counter spoke up with a squeaky voice and said, "I was just trying to get this young man to tell my husband, Leroy, to hang up the gas pump."

After her reply I wanted to hide behind the magazine rack out of embarrassment! I told the customers I was so sorry and I left the store. I was too embarrassed to even buy gas there. I drove to the market down the street for service then I continued on to Houston.

On the trip back to Memphis I devised a plan that would give me a better than average chance of breaking in with this fraternity of controllers.

I would befriend those that appeared open minded.

These guys had interests like woodwork, carpentry, car repairs, and lawn care.

I would learn something about their hobbies so that I could hold a conversation beyond work.

I would definitely make sure I was on point with my knowledge of Air Traffic Control.

When appropriate I would bowl them over with my humor.

And as an added bonus I would be seen carrying my Bible around work. These guys didn't care for outsiders but they had a hidden fear of Christianity.

I am not sure if any of those schemes helped but I did make it.

The acceptance was still distant and combative at times. But I had climbed that mountain. I was in the top 10 percent of incomes in the U.S. Socially I wasn't happy but I could buy most things that I wanted. Up to that point I had lived my whole life watching others like a prisoner behind "the walls". I had broken free from the bullying, the attacks, the put downs, being slighted, being overlooked, being pushed aside, and given hand-me-downs! For the very first time I REALLY REALLY felt like my own man!

"I Be Dog-Gone"

LOATHE AND ENVY have never taken a day off. Even though I had made tremendous inroads, the naysayers and the idiots were not pleased that I was amongst them. A campaign was started to have me removed!

My offenses would be 1: I bought a brand new candy apple red corvette. Driving a new car wasn't the image that my coworkers wanted to see of me. We all made the same money. They bought very big homes and I chose to buy a new car. It was my fantasy and by far the best thing I had ever done for myself!

Offense number 2: My female supervisor was a big Kentucky Wildcat fan. Once she found out that I was pulling for Mississippi State University to beat her team she wanted to have me removed from the facility! I thought it was a bad prank but the joke was squarely on me.

Offense number 3: After watching the Lakers beat the Celtics I was approached by another controller that came to me face to face with a sneer, saying, "All of the Celtics fans are not in Boston!"

I stepped aside and said, "Good for you!" That controller became even more hostile and returned with "You FNG!"

As I recalled from my big Interview, he was calling me a "Freaking Nigger"! I snatched the guy and pinned him up against the wall! After we were separated we were escorted to the chief's office for corrective action!

After talking with the boss, along with other witnesses, I was cleared of my transgressions. The boss assured me that, "FNG" was a military acronym that meant "Freaking New Guy"! I said to the boss that I was so sorry for my misunderstanding. I went on to say that I thought it was one of those racist nursery rhymes like "eeny meeny miny moe."

The boss said, "No sir, it is not!"

I was relieved to know that and I was deeply regretful for reacting the way I had! The boss would leave the controller and me alone to talk things over. I wanted to be a man about what happened! I went on to ask the controller for his forgiveness. I offered to buy him a drink after work. He looked me in the eyes and said, "Your drink won't be necessary. I said what I meant the very first time! eeny meeny miny moe!"

Then he walked out of the room. Maybe I deserved that for putting my hands on him. Either way, he delivered the biggest blow without raising a finger!

Being against University of Kentucky was the worst of my misdeeds and miscues! My female supervisor was very well liked and had unlimited power. Management and coworkers would watch in silence as she proceeded to fire me from my job with dastardly intentions. I had to file a grievance that eventually saved my butt at the eleventh hour! Yet I lost all levels of comfort and confidence working at Memphis Center.

I couldn't get past the fact that I could be destroyed at any time for anything! They wanted a puppet-on-a-string. That just wasn't me! The first chance I got I would leave for greener pastures in Houston, Texas. GO BULLDOGS, DING DONG DAMMIT!

Here Comes the Light!

HAYWARD, ME, AND the gang now had our attention squarely on finding Derrick. Information was coming in quickly that Derrick had been buried beneath the gym. Stopping to catch my breath brought on the chill of the Afghanistan winter. As long as I was active, the cold had seemed no problem. But suddenly I was quivering and dragging quite a bit. I needed to push through my discomfort; otherwise I would be of no real help.

When we got to the gym, the complete structure was gone. It was just layers of wood, sheet metal, and rocks resting two feet above the ground. Somewhere underneath all that wreckage would be Derrick. He was responding but one of his arms had become entangled. We needed to free him quickly to prevent further damage.

As luck would have it the gym was right across from GROUND ZERO. The bomb was placed in a 18-wheeler that was parallel to our workout area.

Our camp was a fortress of three reinforced concrete and dirt walls that stood ten feet tall with a ten by ten foot iron gate. That barrier was a buffer to anything opposite of our barracks. It would have taken a steel train just to breach the gate. Yet, the bomb tore through the walls like an eraser to drawing paper! The iron gate had been blown completely out of sight. Just beyond the big opening was a giant crater that was about fifty yards in circumference and fifteen feet deep. On the other side of that crater was another camp full of foreign national workers. Even though we were fortunate, they were not! They took on many casualties, whereas we had none. Many of the remaining dorms looked as if someone had taken a cake knife and divided up the camp.

It had been more than three hours since the initial attack, yet we were still on our own. Our security was suspect at best. We had to watch each other backs as we hammered away at the sheet metal. It became obvious that we were fighting a losing battle. There was no way that we were going to reach Derrick with the tools that we had on hand. We desperately needed some heavy machinery. So arrangements were made for a crane to come inside to remove steel, sheet metal, wood, and rocks off of Derrick. That was the "Good." The possibility of a Phase II attack loomed even larger! That was the "Bad!" I was getting more and more agitated by the minute. I kept looking out at the crater and seeing locals mulling about. I wasn't comfortable at all! A suicide bomber could have been amongst them. I was the cat on a hot tin roof. I was never standing in the same place. I was undressing any and all faces that I didn't know.

Time crept onward. The cold would bring on a fog and a frost to boot. Our fears were starting to show. No one spoke it but anger and rage filled the air. We were hoping and praying that our request for a crane would be granted. It had been quite awhile since the call went out. Yet our doubts were stronger than our hope.

Privately, I just wasn't sure if Derrick would make it! Secondly, I was afraid of anything new or unvetted coming into our camp. In the meantime another supervisor named Ty took charge of all coordinations. He was also the liaison to the military. Suddenly men with bright lights bearing automatic weapons marched through the open hole. That had to be the Taliban's final push. I was tired, weak, and unarmed with no good places to hide! Life had been a good ride, so I thought! I would know I clocked out fighting to helping others.

Finally, Inside the Wire

I HAD BEEN one of the worker bees' going from situation to situation. Most decisions that were made were not shared with the camp survivors. As I was being blinded by the approaching lights I was looking for cover and a prayer. Not to be outdone two cranes were allowed access into our camp. That had to be a death sandwich.

Like the sequel to a nightmare, life had come to a stop. It was slow motion going forward. I didn't want to run or draw attention but I felt paralyzed, like a deer on the freeway. If these guys were shooting, then we were certainly easy pickings. This had to be Phase II of the Taliban. I just wanted God to make it quick!

None of us knew that Ty had cleared the way for the Quick Reaction Force (QRF) and the cranes to come inside. I wish I had known because I think I went beyond touching cotton! Having that much fear made my state of calm a distant reach. I stood frozen like a kid at a parade! The QRF/Marines combed the grounds looking for terrorists and potential threats. I saw a female soldier with two different colored eyes that reminded me of Dead Eye Red! I think that was my omen of hope!

The cranes bellowed in with thundering roars that were frightening all by themselves. Ty marshaled those super heavy machines into place. They immediately began the removal of the obstacles that lay on top of Derrick .

What had taken hours of our time and effort were suddenly accomplished in a matter of minutes! Derrick was free but he had to be evacuated out of Afghanistan with much haste. He was dehydrated with some internal injuries but ultimately he was going to survive.

Ty continued to work the phones. He instructed all of us to prepare to leave our barracks.

Unbeknownst to any of us, our senior staff had been missing due to being trapped by the explosion. They had been involved in a weekly card game when the blast hit. They were fighting their own battles minus any lighting or medical care. We had become so discombobulated that we overlooked the perils of our superiors. It was so comforting to see them once again! For the first time in my contract life I felt like a battered soldier. My experience was just a smidgen of what some servicemen go through! They will always get much respect from me!

We got bused over to the Military base. We were given our bunks for a temporary stay. It was like being at a funeral. There wasn't a lot of conversations but a few hugs, a few kisses, and a few tears amongst friends. Even I was as muted and as deliberate as a sloth. The only differences were that I could hear and see other employees on their phones making arrangements to exit the Hell of Afghanistan.

Some of us had to work that very night. I didn't have to. I don't know if that was good or bad. It was around 12:00 midnight or Zero Dark Zero Zero according to the military. I knew I wouldn't get any sleep. So I didn't even bother trying. I had my phone out with my finger on speed dial just like everyone else.

Every contractor who has ever done more than one tour has asked himself, "What in the world am I doing?" before returning to this country! Yet there I was in belly of Afghanistan and it was spitting me out like so many before me. Somehow I did calm my nerves well enough to wait a few more days before making a final decision to leave what had become "Hell above Ground"!

Our worksite was very near to our camp and the Military base. We were on the base practically every day for food, haircuts, shopping, business, mail, or for recreation. There was a coalition of forces from around the world at that Post. Our camp was considered outside the Wire (Post) and the Military base was inside the Wire (Post). The

Military post was definitely safer because of the scrutiny, the security, and the soldiers with guns. However, being outside the Wire allowed more freedoms and less constraints of military procedures. Most civilians preferred the camp life even with the risks!

I knew a lot of the servicemen on the Military base. But after the bombing it was like getting to know them all over again. Just the same, I really didn't want to talk to anyone. I felt ashamed but I didn't know how to explain it! Within days my balance and my wits would return.

Little Causes with Big Concerns

I COULD SEE Dylan shaking his head in disbelief. His oval green pupil had narrowed to the size of a pea. He asked me if I had ever experienced other attacks. I said, "Well yes, but not like the Big Explosion!".

Dylan, being Dylan, said, "What do you mean?"

I told him that I was at another camp in Afghanistan named Big Town just two years prior in when there was a bombing outside the gate. I was awakened by the explosion but also because I was levitating above my bed before crashing back into the covers.

Dylan responded with, "Oh Wow, what else?"

I said, "I worked in Iraq right before President Obama's big draw down. Leading up to the military troop reduction, the radicals would unexpectedly and indiscriminately launch rockets onto the base with hopes of killing any members of the military. I was working in the airport tower when the alarms went off; rockets were pelting the base. I could hear whistling noises zooming by the tower. In the distance I saw the impact of missiles hitting the open areas of the camp. Then it dawned on me that I was in the tallest structure on the post. It was definitely time to evacuate that tower!

Now Dylan was working me like a detective. He said, "Let's go back to that outside the fence!"

I said, "You mean,'outside the wire'?"

Dylan said. "Yes, that thing."

"What about it?"

"How does that work?"

"It's basically a contractor thing or mercenary thing. You have these people that are willing to accept the risks of the job yet they want some of the comforts of home. So these big companies create camps with dorms that are hotel-like with heavy protections for those daring workers."

Dylan said, "So, you got to see some of the citizens."

I said, "Yes, plenty of them." I told Dylan that I saw a lot of things that we as Americans take for granted: people living with no electricity, no internet, no heating, no air conditioning, no restrooms, and no drinking water." The citizens around us were very poor yet everybody had a cell phone.

Secondly, we had tons and tons of bottled water--so much water that we were practically tripping over the stuff. Yet, it was one of the biggest gifts that you could give to them.

At one point I interacted with some of the kids on occasion. They would be waiting right outside of our gate. They would ask for anything and everything. Initially, I felt that they should have their butts in class, only to find out that school was a luxury in Afghanistan. There were no truant officers or anyone to give a damn. Secondly, every day was survival. So if a kid brought home a dollar or a package of water then he had probably added more to the table than his parents.

Nothing placed parenting into perspective like watching a four-year-old kid walking a two-year-old hand-in-hand along a busy road while M-Raps, Armored Tanks, and Humvees went speeding by. I had no kinship but it would scare the hell out of me! I would see little kids walking those dangerous roads day after day all alone as if traffic wasn't an issue.

Against my better judgment, I started giving out bottles of water. No doubt the kids would trade them for money or other items at the local market. That move only created more demands and more needy kids. I would also buy them chocolate bars, cookies, and soft drinks, which made them happy, hyper, and overly aggressive. I should have known better! But just like any American kid, they loved the stuff. I would watch the three and four-year-olds push their way to the front of the line! I even made the mistake of hugging one of the smaller ones and, like magic, I missed those moments with my own children. But it really gave them a human face! We had pegged them as "terrorists in training" but they were just little kids in need. In my head they had become my boys. Somehow I wanted to protect them. The men would prey on stray boys for their gratification! It was a taboo for men to be around unmarried women but who would question boys being around men! I often wondered if my guys were safe! I didn't speak the language so I didn't know how to go there. And sadly, nothing legally would have been done about it.

I became their favorite, whereas my co-workers got the middle finger and a few swear words on their way to work. The kids would give me high fives and handshakes. They would do the stuff that my kids used to do like touching my clothing or leaning up against me! They did just about anything to signify that I was special to them. And of course they had me fooled.

It got to where they would block my vehicle if they saw me leaving the gate. Then they would place orders for things they wanted me to bring back from the military base—items like bottles of water, chocolate bars, cookies, money, and even watches. Of course, I would laugh as I drove off, thinking how bold and how demanding they had become!

As I made it back to camp from the military post I had bought enough for the four kids who greeted me on my way out. But when I returned there were eight or more of them waiting. I served these kids snacks on a constant basis for six straight months and sometimes twice a week.

I gave out the treats to the youngest and I promised the older ones that I would take care of them on my following trip. But as I closed the door to my truck and pulled away, I was being bombarded with bricks, dirt, cans, and even some of the water bottles I had given out. My truck got a hell of a lot of damage on a hot sunny day! That display stopped my acts of charity from that point onward.

Dylan was laughing and laughing at me. He then asked if I saw anything else out of the ordinary.

I replied, "Oh yes! On flights back to my worksite I would see different nationalities of teenagers by the dozens traveling to Afghanistan as a final stop. I'm sure they weren't going there for work or to attend college. One: Work was extremely hard to find. In order to get a job, their resume had to state that, "They knew someone who knew somebody that knew someone who shot somebody!" Otherwise, there was no chance at employment. And Two: No one went to Afghanistan for advance education. So therefore, they had to be reinforcements for the military!"

Then Dylan pulled out the million dollar question. He asked, "What was your final decision after the bombing?"

I said, "Dylan, I knew that was coming. But I'm not sure you're going to like all of my answers."

He said, "Oh, you have answers!"

"Of course I do."

Dylan, then shot back, "I have been with you from story to story. I have heard your moments of death and destruction. We have drunk ourselves from intoxication to sobriety, then to intoxication again. I would never judge you, my friend."

I suddenly felt a relief and a bond. Dylan had been great therapy for me. I would even say that Dylan had become a friend. I had emptied my soul. I rolled to the side of my massage table and said, "Dylan, what we do have in common are the facts that we have fewer tomorrows than we have yesterdays. You might not like my answers but so be it!"

After walking around and searching myself I came to the realization that I wasn't ready to accept getting older and sitting on a porch! I was addicted to the international lifestyle. And I didn't care for the politics of home.

Then Dylan came back with, "It is what it is. I'm still not here to judge you."

Holy Crap!

I SAID, "DYLAN, since you have been digging into my big adventure, I have some added bonuses for you."

Dylan smirked at me. "Really, what are they?"

I said, "Dylan, I used to tease my daughter about using mobile potties! It was quite the amusement for me. I would dare her to enter one. I even told her about the outhouses of the South. I went into sordid detail about being able to see the diet of the person that used the facility before you. I told her that she could visit that same home years later and that outhouse may be in a different location on the same property. She didn't find my pranks or the conversations very funny!

"I even took my four-year-old son into a mobile potty during an emergency only to have him rat me out to his mom when we got home. He was completely traumatized by the experience! I even laughed about that. Then I ended up in Afghanistan, where mobile potties are the normal when it comes to relief at my worksite. Each time I entered one I couldn't help but think about my daughter and my son getting karma times a million on old dad. I would sarcastically laugh at myself, regretting that I picked on them!

Some of the experiences were all too memorable! There was the "blue butt." That's when you got splashed by the retaining water. It would leave a stained color residue on your butt. There was the "stall call!" That was when you accidentally dropped your phone down the toilet while trying to talk or text. There was the "open door policy!" That was when the persons were either too tall or too big to fit inside the toilet so they would leave the door open while doing their business! There was "the sauna." Everyone got "the sauna" treatment! We had to use these things in the deserts with temperatures well above 100 degrees. You would sweat so profusely that everyone would know where you had been! Sometimes there was a combination of "the sauna and the open door policy." That depended on the person's size and the temperature outside. No one attempted to read the newspaper or a magazine while during their business. Then there was the "butt breaker." That was when it was so cold that your butt stuck to the seat! Finally, the most disgusting was the "snow cone." No one talked about the "snow cone." It was far too gruesome for everyone's comfort. However, this was when the manure was taller than the toilet seat!

Dylan turned green and begged me to stop. But I wasn't finished!

I told him that I really appreciated the comforts and cleanliness of decent facilities after that. Of course, we would try to refrain usage until back at camp! But the stress on our faces provided just another opportunity to tease each other!"

Dylan was smiling again and still a bit curious about my crappy conversation. He said, "What else you got?"

I chuckled. "There was this one incident where this guy ran out of T.P. so he cut his underwear up as a substitute. We all suffered that day! Dylan chimed, "Oh my, Wow, Oh my!"

I then added, "Yet, we preferred the mobile potties over the airport facilities!"

Dylan stated, "Goodness, you are kidding!"

"Dylan, honestly I'm not! But I will flush this conversation and move ahead." At that point Dylan thanked me! I could see that he had enough.

Take Me to the House!

DYLAN LET OUT a deep sigh and continued to make comments. He said," Man, you walked a goat rope!"

I said,"Dylan, indeed I did".

He then added,"The bombing, the aunt, the schizophrenia, the jobs, the women, and your dad!

Out of nowhere Dylan asked about my mom.

I said, "Dylan, that may be my deepest gaping hole of them all."

He passed me a double shot of rum. He could tell that it wasn't easy for me.

Yet I thought I was still ok, so I said, "Dylan, you may need that drink as I finish up! Mr. Dylan Owen, let me take it home."

He had been a good audience. Now it was time to give him some relief from the voyages of my life.

Smart on the Inside, Crazy on the Outside

BECAUSE OF MOM'S disorder I was sure she was a complete loss. Even at an early age I had no confidence in her ability to be anymore than a sideshow.

In the second grade our teachers sent home a memo for parents to participate with their kids in a talent show. Somewhere between the sloppiness of Bennie or myself, a note about this event was discovered by our mom. Bennie and I went into overdrive trying to convince her that she shouldn't go and for sure shouldn't participate. Mom was having none of it.

We had no skit, or play, or act. We had nothing to suggest either. None of us could sing! Bennie could dance. But I definitely didn't want Mom trying to sing or dance! Once again I was completely paralyzed. Bennie and me were totally dumbfounded! Just the thought of Mom being involved gave us anxiety attacks.

We tried every lie and every excuse for her not to show up! But to Mom this was her big moment.

On the night of the notorious event I kept asking Bennie, "What are you going to do?" Hell, I wasn't even sure what I was going to do! Mom was excited and determined to go through with her own theater. There had been no rehearsal. There was no dry run! We had no idea what she had in mind. This was a play for the kids with adult help. Not the one woman show that was going to be "Mom"!

When we got to the school Mom made sure to keep Bennie

nearby. I think she knew I was a stray cat so she didn't even bother trying to control me. I was wandering around looking for a good place to hide. I was picturing all the embarrassment that would ensue before, during, and after her fiasco.

Mom, Bennie, and I took the stage behind the curtains. Mind you I was tearing slightly because of what appeared to be the dismal end of my social life. As Mom and Bennie went to center stage I found a spot that I hoped shielded me completely from the audience. When the curtains rolled back, there was a low rumble, snickers, and a few spots of laughter. My heart was definitely beating louder than the audience!

After Principal Shell Shock signaled for the audience to settle down. Mom went on to recite the Gettysburg address dynamically and in flawless form. I mean she did it with no practice. There was a raucous standing ovation. Even though I was a little piss-ant, that night I was never more proud of her! Of course that glow was only temporary because the next day she was up to her old tricks of humiliating and shaming me. But for that solitary moment it felt so good to see your mom admired!

I stopped talking just to see if Dylan was consciously with me. As a matter-of-fact he was. He even made the statement: "Way to go, girl"!

I shook my head in agreement, then I gulped down a large part of my hooch. I took a deep breath and stared out into the distance at the deep blue sea. The clouds had moved in and the sun was drifting away. There wasn't much of a breeze left to keep us cool. Only a few speckled drops of rain began. Even the circling birds had taken a rest. Quite a number of tourists had nudged closer to our tables. My stories had unexpectedly taken a toll on me! I had an audience at my worst possible moment. This time I had boxed my own self in. I tried to pretend and deflect toward Dylan. Yet he sensed my trouble. He kept shaking me and asking if I was ok! I had no answers for him. I grabbed a beach towel and buried my head. The tide had rolled in. I had promised to finish, yet I needed a moment just within myself! I was trying to make sense of it all. Methodically, I grimly bit my lip to hold back my emotion. No doubt the end of\b had come!

Jb

The Walls Stand Silent Now!

YOU SEE, MOM passed in February of 2017. There I was, trying to get the brothers together for her final respects. Bennie was the toughest one to get on page for her service. He wanted nothing to do with me, being that I never treated him like the King he thought he was programmed to be. However, he still had that liquid courage. He had gassed up before coming to see me. He was reeking of alcohol like a bad cologne! He tried to stick it to me even at that moment of sorrow. He told me that the suits I had given Ezell had been stolen. Like an echo in the room, I repeated his statement. "How in the hell do you steal Ezell's suits?" I said.

He looked at me with a gleeful smile and said, "You get a key and the key fits the lock!"

Yes, he suckered me in like a dummy! Then I returned Bennie a look that could have twisted steel! He had stolen Ezell's clothing and was smiling at me about it! I wanted to tell him, "You may be drunk but I'm still your Kryptonite!"

Dylan and the crowd waited patiently. I had echoed in and out but now recovered. The wheel was mine again. I said, "Dylan, it was an unexpected call out of nowhere. Mom had been sick for some time; but she, Aunt Kathy, and my brothers never told me of her illness." Aunt Kathy had persuaded Mom to accept her fate without proper medical attention.

Of course, I was as angry as a bucking bull but that wasn't going to bring her back! It was time to let go and let God have her.

Everything around Mom's life had always been erratic and

unpredictable. Her funeral was no different. While I was sitting on the front row wiping away my sad tears, shaking like a feather, and spinning out of control, Bennie raised his fist as if to say, "Charge!"

It took a minute for me to wrap my head around that gesture.

As pastor Lloyd was giving the eulogy I was thinking of his sermon from Matthew 8:23-27. I just wanted to hear him say, "Peace, be still" one last time!

Then I moved on to reminiscing through Mom's biggest and boldest stunts.

I saw Mom riding her bicycle in the middle of the street to purposely hold up traffic; Mom carrying a sheer umbrella that shut out no sun; Mom doing donuts at the bus stop on her bicycle; Mom chasing kids on her bicycle; Mom wearing a blond wig incognito; Mom doing two to three low passes by the house before finally stopping at our apartment; Mom crossing the road to deliberately force people off the sidewalk; And Mom going nose to nose with "the wall." Memories of her will dance in my head until the end of my own time!

I know that mom will continue to fight those ghosts, devils, dead dogs, and haints with all her fury. But from here on, those evil spirits won't have me to distract her or slow her down. "Do your thing, Mom! CHARGE and Give them Hell! I shall love you forever!"

My friend now appeared stoic! He had downed the drink that he previously offered me. It was as if he wasn't sure where he was. He was suddenly blotting would-be sweat like a pig in the desert.

I said, "Dylan, I'm here."

"You are here, where"?

I said, "I am in Thailand."

"I know, hell, I'm in Thailand too."

"No Dylan, that's my story." He then went "Man, oh God. What the Hell?" Then he said, "You have been screwing with me, right?"

I deflected again. "Dylan, no one leaves Thailand without a smile. I'm sure you know all the best bars and best restaurants. Why don't we make it a night out after the ladies finish my back rub."

Dylan agreed while occasionally glancing up in wonderment.

I said, "Life just happens! Nothing is promised and mostly it's never fair! But life will keep coming at you from many different angles whether you're ready or not."

Dylan smiled faintly. I think he gave me a pass on my bullshit, or he was just too drunk to even care. We staggered off to our separate condos followed by four ladies that I had promised to marry every step of the way!

Acknowledgments

I HAVE TO thank God for protecting me as I fought for my life in that mighty ordeal. Without his mercy I would not have been able to share my survival or the history of my life.

I'd like to dedicate this book in memory of my mom. Her passing was the final motivation to share my stories.

I have to thank my dad, mom, brother and sister for being so accepting. You all have been awesome from day one. Honestly, I don't know how we did it but we did! I will forever love you all.

I'd like to thank the author, the speaker, and the president of Georgia Writer's museum, John P. Dennis ("Men raised by Women," "The Straw-man," and "The Blank Check") for helping me to develop this book. John was the hand and the ear that steadied my drive to write it. He was far more than a coach for me. He was a friend and a counselor when I needed one. I can never thank him enough! I have never met a talent like John P. Dennis.

I want to honor the troops and the contractors that have lost their lives in Afghanistan. They shall never be forgotten!

Bio: Harold Phifer

HAROLD PHIFER WAS born and raised in Columbus, Mississippi. All of his first 25 years were solidly spent inside his home state. After graduating from Mississippi State University and Jackson State University he went on to work for the Federal Aviation Administration (FAA) for 23 years as an Air Traffic Controller. He eventually left the FAA and began work as an international contractor where he has done numerous tours in Iraq and Afghanistan.